The Evils of Polygyny

THE EASTON LECTURES

The Evils of Polygyny

Evidence of Its Harm to Women, Men, and Society

Rose McDermott

Edited by Kristen Renwick Monroe

Commentary by
B. J. Wray, Robert Jervis, and Valerie Hudson

Cornell University Press
Ithaca and London

First published 2018 by Cornell University Press

Printed in the United States of America

Library of Congress Cataloging-in-Publication Data

Names: McDermott, Rose, 1962– author. | Monroe, Kristen Renwick, 1946– editor. | Container of (work): Wray, B. J., 1968– Canadian polygamy reference. | Container of (work): Jervis, Robert, 1940– Polygyny, pastoralism, and violence against women. | Container of (work): Hudson, Valerie M., 1958– Deep structure of collective security.
Title: The evils of polygyny : evidence of its harm to women, men, and society / Rose McDermott ; edited by Kristen Renwick Monroe ; commentary by B.J. Wray, Robert Jervis, and Valerie Hudson.
Description: Ithaca : Cornell University Press, 2018. | Includes bibliographical references and index. |
Identifiers: LCCN 2017052531 (print) | LCCN 2017053204 (ebook) | ISBN 9781501714849 (pdf) | ISBN 9781501714757 (ret) | ISBN 9781501718038 | ISBN 9781501718038 (cloth ; alk. paper) | ISBN 9781501718045 (pbk ; alk. paper)
Subjects: LCSH: Polygyny. | Male domination (Social structure) | Women—Violence against.
Classification: LCC HQ997.5 (ebook) | LCC HQ997.5 .M33 2018 (print) | DDC 306.84/23—dc23
LC record available at https://lccn.loc.gov/2017052531

To our mothers, Kathleen McDermott and Gertrude Renwick Monroe, whose generation paved the way for a fuller inclusion of women into public and political life, and whose personal support and love encouraged us to follow our own paths.

To Kristi's daughter, Chloe. May she live in a world where women are valued and cherished as equal members of society.

Polygyny: Marriage between one man and multiple wives.
Polygamy: Having more than one spouse.
Polyandry: Marriage between one woman and multiple men.

Polygamy is a broader concept than are polygyny, which refers to situations where one man has multiple wives, and polyandry, which refers to one woman with multiple husbands. It is frequently but erroneously assumed that polygamy refers only to the marriage of one man to multiple women. Most likely this confusion arises since polygyny is more common—or at least more newsworthy—than is polyandry. In current media discussions, polygamy most frequently is used to refer to North American religious sects that, in fact, practice only polygyny. In the contemporary world and among modern countries that permit polygamy, polygyny is typically the only form of multiple marriage practiced. The bulk of the discussion here is thus restricted to polygyny, not only because it is vastly more prevalent, but also because the harms documented here do not necessarily apply to cases of polyandry. Therefore, it would be erroneous to overattribute the ills discussed here to situations where polygyny does not apply.

CONTENTS

THE EVILS OF POLYGYNY

INTRODUCTION

Polygyny and the Treatment of Women

Kristen Renwick Monroe

Allala was a beautiful young woman, a Somali student in one of my courses at the University of California, Irvine (UCI), a refugee from the ongoing bloodshed that has plagued her country since the 1980s. Allala had been born in Somalia but fled because of the civil war and lived in Saudi Arabia and Kenya, where a refugee agency recognized how intelligent she was and arranged for her to come to UCI on a fellowship. Allala was an excellent student, and we became friendly over the course of the term. Allala spent Thanksgiving of 2015 with us and was in and out of my office during the rest of the year. In one of our conversations she told me about her life and what was expected of her as a young Somali woman, fortunate enough to receive a wonderful education.[1]

Allala was one of ten siblings. Her older sister was already married, living in the Persian Gulf with her husband, two children, and several of

---

1. I have changed the name and some of the basic facts of Allala's life story, to protect her privacy. I appreciate her permission to use her story to illustrate the personal aspect of polygyny.

her siblings. Allala's father had taken a second wife and had four or five additional children with his second wife. He was pondering whether or not to take a third wife. Allala explained to me that she was expected to take care of all of these people, all her siblings and the half-siblings, in addition to both her parents. Further, she was expected to contract an arranged marriage and have children of her own, whom she also would have to support. As this volume goes to press, Allala has married and is agonizing over whether to have children immediately—as her husband wishes—or to continue her graduate education first.

Allala's situation was fresh in my mind as I read through this volume on polygyny. She brought a human face to a practice that is widespread and overpowering for the individuals who live in it. This book addresses polygyny in the context of a broader subject, one often taboo in political discussions: how we treat women, especially in what is known as the Third World. McDermott and her coauthors boldly address this question on several important fronts. In doing so, they venture into areas in international relations, foreign and domestic policy, and human rights without regard for a political correctness that can stifle honest discussion of divisive topics. Nowhere is this intellectual bravery more evident than in the first chapter, in which McDermott speaks from her heart as a scholar who has devoted nearly two decades of her professional life to studying this pernicious system of marriage. Every member of Congress and the U.S. Department of State should read this chapter, which documents McDermott's personal interest in polygyny as a topic, how polygyny relates to violence toward women, and how McDermott herself became involved in the collection of statistics on women throughout the world, an extraordinary data set, free to all scholars, and known as WomanStats.[2] The first chapter provides a fascinating intellectual history of an idea, an introduction into policy and law and how one person can influence a field in profound ways. Chapter 1

---

2. Based at Texas A&M, the WomanStats Project (www.womanstats.org) is an institutional and donor-funded research and database project consisting of statistical data on the status of women and children around the world. Under the leadership of Valerie M. Hudson, WomanStats allows scholars to connect data on women with data on the security of states, using a wide range of metrics. WomanStats offers both qualitative and quantitative information on over three hundred indicators of women's status in 174 countries with populations of at least two hundred thousand. This online data archive is free.

thus also makes excellent reading for anyone contemplating the scholarly life, providing insights on how interdisciplinary work can be done, how scholars can affect people's lives, and some of the normative and ethical concerns of a scholar in a multicultural world in which the concern for sensitivity brought by political correctness can stifle free and frank discussion and unapologetic and scrupulously honest research.

Chapter 2 lays the methodological groundwork for the later empirical analysis. It also highlights David Easton's concern with methodology, and in particular Easton's awareness of the extent to which the models we employ to analyze political activity vary and can shape the substantive findings at which we arrive. McDermott and her coauthor, Peter K. Hatemi, note how many critical developments in political-attitude research and survey methodology grew out of research methods and theories that originated in clinical and developmental psychology. While this approach was superseded for a while by behaviorist and rational choice approaches, earlier models of clinical and developmental psychology are now being integrated into recent approaches from a wide range of areas, from behavior genetics to cognitive neuroscience. The intellectual history of the use of developmental and clinical models of psychology and their application to a wide range of new types of substantive work in social and political science will prove extremely useful both for students of the discipline and for more advanced scholars interested in how older techniques can be revised and updated to work well in a wide range of political science venues, as it does here for the later analysis of polygyny.

After laying the groundwork methodologically, McDermott and her coauthor Jonathan Cowden begin a more formal analysis (chapter 3) by addressing the difficulties of discussing polygyny in the context of the West's uneasy relations with the Muslim world. An often-cited explanation for much of these uneasy tensions grew out of the conviction that, after 9/11, the Muslim world "hates us." Since the destruction of the World Trade Center and the crash at the Pentagon that precipitated the war on terror, politicians, pundits, scholars, policymakers, and other members of the interested public have wondered: "Why do they dislike us so? What have we done to incur such anger?" While acknowledging the extent to which much of the fabled "clash of civilizations" is actually fueled by disputes over material resources—land and power, most particularly—and dramatically divergent political cultures and institutions, McDermott and her coauthor focus on what is often a neglected part of the discussion: the extent to which problems between the West and the Muslim world reflect a fundamental tension over the appropriate role of women in society. This clash emerges independently of economic and political contests, although such issues often serve to fuel such conflicts. Because Western values often encourage a foundation of at least legal equality between the sexes, threats to the assumed sociopolitical dominance of men in areas that strongly espouse these traditions provoke systematic hostility and opposition. As a result, the authors in this volume make clear, we are arguing about the wrong questions.

> Rather than counterposing East against West, arguing about the clash of civilizations in the prototypical Huntington sense (1997), the critical concern should actually revolve around the sources and consequences of violence by men toward women as the root of conflict both within and between nations. (McDermott and Cowden, chap. 3, p. 53)

An underlying theme of this volume, then, holds that unless and until we address the question of violence toward women, including that of a system that tells young women—like Allala—that they must marry whom their elders tell them to and devote their entire lives to serving and caring for others, we will not resolve a whole series of conflicts that plague the contemporary world and that manifest themselves in different ways.

This provocative third chapter expands McDermott's personal statement to raise a whole series of difficult questions on this topic:

> What are some of the origins of the violence that men direct toward women? Is it simply rooted in male sexual desire for women and the anger and frustration that may result when men hold women responsible for their own drives? Or do men seek to control women simply because they [men] are physically and financially stronger and they are able to get away with exerting power over those with fewer resources? Alternatively, does male violence emerge from a much broader array of social incentives and permissions? And what are the consequences of such violence, not only for women and children, but also for the men who instigate it and for the societies that sanction it? These patterns of violence often begin in the home and serve as models for the assumed hierarchical relationships between the sexes, as well as implicit endorsement for dominance, coercion, and violence as the

proper form of conflict resolution in society more broadly. (McDermott and Cowden, chap. 3, p. 53)

The claim that female financial and social independence are feared because of the threat they pose to the cultural values, status, and personal power of men, especially in developing regions of the world, will not go unchallenged. Indeed, it well may anger many. The scope of the revolution McDermott and Cowden identify confronts stark reality, and the scope of the challenge is vast, since emancipating women will erode male control over their own families. Often this will result in shifts that are potentially humiliating culturally and emotionally painful for men, especially those men emanating from a tradition of strong patriarchy. In short, as McDermott and her coauthors demonstrate, again and again:

> The prospect of liberated women threatens male status. Further, it often also threatens the position of senior women in these developing societies, women who are allowed to dominate junior women, such as daughters and daughters-in-law, as well as junior men, including sons. (McDermott and Cowden, chap. 3, p. 53)

We should be clear, McDermott and her coauthor write: It is not just men who jealously guard a culture that oppresses women; women actively participate in such repression by refusing to relinquish control over those few cultural areas to which they have been assigned by men, including circumscribing the activities of their female family members. The prospect of female emancipation therefore provides a potent source of male—and sometimes even female—objection to more secular or democratic movements, particularly in more patriarchal societies.

The unflinching analysis of the problem McDermott and her co-authors present reveals how the process of control is exacerbated by the common practice of patrilocality, whereby women move to the town, village, or home of their husbands, often leaving behind the fathers, brothers, or uncles who might protect them if they lived closer to home. Without such protection from family members, the only prospect many women have for protection from abusive relatives is to give birth to sons, who are valued by the father's family. (I think here of Allala's sister, living far from home and her familial support system. She does not drive a car and is unable to leave the apartment without her husband. In addition to her own two children, Allala's sister also has taken two of her siblings to live with her, thus serving as mother to four children and with little by way of a support system.) These sons, in turn, may prove loyal to these mothers. But such a family structure further erodes the bonds between husband and wife, since the husband's primary loyalty to a woman often remains with his mother rather than with his wife or his daughters. Such a privileging of parent–child bonds over the marital bond further diminishes the possibility for creating models of equality between the sexes for children of such unions.

The analysis of patriarchal cultures, and their patrilocality and polygynist family structures, links the increasing risk for political violence against women to increased levels of many forms of violence in and across these areas. McDermott and Cowden make a convincing case that men's desire for patriarchal control of women is not so arbitrary that it can be blown away by a good breath of Western logic, education, or liberalism. Its roots in strong traditions and structures, often endorsed by religious beliefs, privilege male power and dominance in all aspects of life. The violent effects emerge from the widespread lifestyle of patriarchy, polygyny, and patrilocality and therefore have continuing significance in many countries today where such practices continue to dominate cultural and economic traditions. McDermott and Cowden trace these origins of male power and note their consequences for the lives and status of women throughout the developing world.

Their discussion of the independent effects of patriarchy and polygyny is followed by a detailed analysis of the impact of these forces on a wide variety of manifestations of violence toward women and children using data derived from the WomanStats Project (www.womanstats.org). Chapter 3 concludes by considering the challenges faced by policymakers and human rights advocates who wish to begin to redress such gender inequalities.

Chapter 4 confronts a critical aspect of the common practice worldwide, linking polygyny to negative outcomes for women and children throughout the world. McDermott and her coauthors—Michael Dickerson, Steve Fish, Danielle Lussier, and Jonathan Cowden—note that attitudes regarding additional wives offer a microcosm into decision-making authority within the family and thus also echo larger societal values reflecting the prevalence of patriarchal structures. Using an experimental manipulation embedded in nationally representative samples, McDermott and her co-authors examine the effects of a previous wife's opinion on approval for a husband taking a second wife, among both men and women. Chapter 4 thus compares results obtained from a total of 9,203 subjects drawn from Lebanon, Jordan, Uganda, Indonesia, Mongolia, and two provinces in India: Bihar and the Punjab.

Chapter 4 asks whether the sex of a respondent affects their response to the experimental manipulation. Here McDermott and her coauthors find surprising and significant differences in attitudes toward polygyny that differ by region and speak to significant variance in women's empowerment and equality around the globe. If wives do not favor their husband's taking of further wives, this seems strong and stark evidence that they find polygyny untenable and unwanted as a form of living.

The volume concludes with comments by B. J. Wray, the lawyer who used McDermott's work in a successful reference trial on polygyny at the Supreme Court of British Columbia,[3] and by two academics—Valerie M. Hudson and Robert Jervis—who are well known in international relations and who locate the importance of these Easton Lectures for international politics.

Since this is the first Easton Lecture, an afterword describes the lecture series and notes the intellectual legacy of David Easton. I am delighted that Cornell University Press will be publishing these lectures and am pleased to introduce the lecture series with the work of Rose McDermott.

---

3. Wray was part of a legal team that defended the constitutionality of the prohibition of polygamy on behalf of the attorney general of Canada. Beginning in the fall of 2010, the chief justice of the Supreme Court of British Columbia presided over this proceeding into the constitutionality of Canada's criminal prohibition of polygamy. McDermott's work was used as part of a voluminous amount of evidentiary records on the impact of polygamy on individuals, communities, and nation-states. The court ultimately found that, as a marital institution, polygamy is inherently harmful.

1

The Meaning and Meanness of Polygyny

Rose McDermott

I never expected to spend so much of my research career investigating the practice of polygyny. In graduate school, I was a student of the incomparable Amos Tversky, spending my time working on prospect theory, risk-taking, and how uncertainty and ambiguity affect decision making about weapons procurement and other more traditional measures of violence and destruction. I did not work on issues related to gender at all; frankly, I was not all that interested in them. And then, of course, life happened, and I began to see how pervasive, powerful, and subtle personal violence is between men and women, and how these seemingly small processes are manifested in much larger ways on the world stage and compromise security for everyone.

Like any important journey, my exploration of polygyny, and other aspects of sex differences in aggression, was never a solo effort. I was blessed by transformative and towering intellectual mentors, in particular Richard Wrangham and Leda Cosmides, who helped shape how I came to think about the meaning, purpose, and function of such activities. I have been lucky to have numerous collaborators who have shared this path of inquiry with me, most importantly Valerie Hudson, who led the way in documenting how micro processes in the household can engender macrolevel security concerns. So, much to my surprise, I have spent over fifteen years collecting and analyzing data examining the impact of polygyny on outcomes of violence related to women and children. This chapter tells a bit of that story in service of communicating the much more important findings that this work brought to light, ending with some of the conclusions I have reached as a result of my work on gender, security, and polygyny.

The Origins of the Inquiry

I can date the start of this research agenda, unlike many areas of intellectual interest, to a particular moment in time: the terrorist attacks on September 11, 2001, and a specific conversation with Richard Wrangham that grew out of it. I was a postdoctoral fellow at the Kennedy School at Harvard that year, on leave from my position as a junior faculty member in the Government Department at Cornell. In fact, I had flown out of Logan the morning before the searing events of 9/11, on September 10, to return to Ithaca for a short visit. As those who were present at the time can easily recall, Boston was a very tense city, having been the airport from which the planes that executed the attacks departed. Al Gore, who had recently lost the presidential bid despite a higher percentage of the popular vote, came to Harvard to ask a dozen prominent faculty from various places and disciplines what had precipitated the attacks—"why they hated us"—and what could be done to prevent similar attacks in the future. Many scholars of international relations, including myself, would not have constructed the question in that way, although some like Samuel Huntington might have, but that was nonetheless how the question was posed by an influential policymaker at the time. I note this only because one of the most important lessons that Amos Tversky taught me was that the way you frame your questions determines the kinds of answers you can uncover. Learning to reframe the question thus becomes a critical aspect of undertaking creative work. Regardless of the cause, the question of how to deter future terrorists' attacks remains a pressing problem for

American foreign policy despite the intervening years of war and conflict designed to reduce such threat.

During the meeting with Gore, Richard Wrangham, a professor of human evolutionary biology at Harvard, was invited to the discussion along with nine other male faculty and two female faculty, one of whom was Carol Gilligan, author of *In a Different Voice*. Everyone went around the room to say what they thought the reasons for the attacks were. The answers ranged from an objection to capitalism to religious, historical, and cultural difference. When it was his turn, Richard said he thought the problem really lay in polygyny and the male desire to control female productive and reproductive capacity. He suggested we needed to investigate the social structures that controlled women and that polygyny was one of those structures, along with other processes such as pastoralism. These structures combined to support patriarchal structures around the world. As a result, men would do a great deal to defend their privileged position against societies that sought to provide mechanisms that allowed for greater female emancipation, which threatened their social status as well as economic prospects. Apparently he got a bunch of blank stares, with Carol Gilligan the only one to nod in agreement. When all the members were asked to submit two-page summaries of their ideas, Richard did not receive a response to his ideas and was curious about why his notion did not spark more interest.

I happened to be in his lab a few days after that for a meeting, and he told me this story over the copy machine while he was making copies of his report. He speculated that part of the skepticism may result from the fact that there was not a lot of data on the topic. He wondered out loud how hard it would be to collect data on rates and practices of polygyny around the world. I immediately responded, "It can't be *that* hard. I bet I can get some." Little did I know that I would be embarking on a decade's research agenda.

Because the origin of my undertaking is so closely associated with the terrorist attacks of 9/11, an additional and critical point is worth noting here, at the inception of this book. Political correctness as well as the legitimate respect for religious freedom and tolerance can make people reluctant to talk about religion and specific religious practices that may flow from and be associated with particular religions. There is no question that everyone should be free to practice whatever religion they choose;

that right is instantiated in the founding documents of the United States among other places. But as social scientists, we cannot and should not shy away from the recognition of patterns and associations. Indeed, the discovery of such relationships constitutes the foundational basis of all true science. When such scientific practices are followed objectively, without prior political sanction, it becomes possible to uncover some of the ways in which beliefs have consequences regardless of who practices them or why. As this entire volume demonstrates, polygyny is unequivocally one of those behaviors that has negative consequences regardless of who practices it or why. Even if atheists practice polygyny, it still has the same negative consequences. Thus, while the 9/11 issue may have motivated the search for data on polygyny, we clearly recognized from the outset that the concern was broader than any given religion, and we sought to identify patterns of consequences that might follow from the behavior itself, regardless of any demographic characteristics of those who practice it.

Definitions and Background

In common parlance, when most people talk about polygyny, they use the term interchangeably with "polygamy." Yet, although the meanings overlap somewhat, the various terms technically refer to different things. For example, polyandry is rare, occurring in only a few places in Nepal and a few politically oriented communities in the United States, including a prominent group in Seattle. When polyandry does exist in traditional societies, it always occurs concomitant with polygyny, and often takes place between wealthy or high-status women and lower-status brothers (over a third of cases of polyandry are fraternal) who then often take additional wives as they themselves become wealthier. Polyandry does not cause widespread social problems when it occurs.

In contrast, polygyny remains more common than many people realize, occurring to some degree in over 83 percent of 849 societies that have been studied worldwide, as opposed to four absolute cases of polyandry in those same places (Gray 1998). Polygyny too is often sororal, meaning men marry sisters, since that often reduces the rates and intensity of interwife violence. More important, polygyny provides a single root for many extremely diverse sources of violence against women and children, as the empirical work in this volume demonstrates in painstaking detail. Therefore, I speak about polygyny because my concern is exclusively with the much more common case of men having many wives, rather than the much rarer instance of women having many husbands. I do not want anyone to assume that the findings presented here that relate to polygyny apply to polyandry, for there is no evidence whatsoever that they do.

It is important to think about polygyny in larger terms of human reproductive systems. In popular usage, people often conflate the social and breeding use and meaning of the term "polygamy." "Breeding" refers to whom one has children with, while "bonding" refers to social relationships. Theoretically and personally, these represent orthogonal dimensions, although of course they often overlap. But we all know people who have sex with people they may not like and who love people, even romantically, with whom they do not have sex. I want to be absolutely clear that the negative findings I present below relate to the impact of polygyny on reproductive systems of breeding and having and raising children. I make no claim about the consequences of the kind of serial monogamy, or indeed parallel polygyny, that is common in modern societies regarding social bonding strategies. These patterns also may potentiate the kind of interpersonal violence that I document below, but my evidence primarily speaks to the consequences of breeding within polygynous structures as opposed to monogamous ones. Therefore, I should not be understood to be making any normative claims about the value of plural sexual partners in a purely social context. That is for individuals to decide for themselves; but once children are involved—and they almost inevitably are in societies patterned on permissible polygynous structures—the negative consequences I detail below inevitably result from the logic of human reproductive systems and become endemic. They also then inexorably exert the kind of disastrous widespread macro outcomes I delineate in the empirical work presented in chapter 3.

Why and how does polygyny exert such pronounced and numerous negative outcomes? The key to understanding this impact lies in the math of sex ratio imbalances. When a man takes many wives, there are fewer women available for other men. That means that while almost all women are married, many polygynously, the majority of men are monogamous, since they cannot afford more than one wife. However, because of the sex ratio imbalance imposed by plural marriage, many men, often a majority, have no wives at all in societies where polygyny is prevalent. For example, in one study looking at eighteen African countries between 1921 and 1951, 39 percent of wives were in monogamous relationships, while 39 percent of husbands were in polygamous relationships; conversely, 61 percent of wives were in polygynous relationships, while 61 percent of husbands were in monogamous ones (van de Berghe 1987). This imbalance is the crux of what precipitates widespread societal effects of violence based on individual patterns of sexual behavior.

In many advanced industrial societies, which tend to be both large and complex, monogamy is socially imposed and sometimes even supported by state structures offering various benefits such as family leave. Additionally, in many foraging societies, monogamy is ecologically enforced, since almost no one can afford more than one wife under subsistence level conditions of survival. Polygyny may be allowed but is difficult for any but very few to achieve in practice. Now it becomes natural to ask the next question about why women would agree to be the nth wife as opposed to being in a monogamous marriage. This is because, in many cases, the woman remains much better off financially being the sequential wife of a very wealthy man than being the single wife of a very poor one.

Aside from the self-evident sexual perquisite of having multiple wives, polygyny serves additional important functions for men. Men again gain control over both female productive as well as reproductive labor, and they get status from other men because of their ability to control more daughters, which they can then sell or barter to other men for additional wealth and privilege. Women are limited by reproductive biology in how many children they can give birth to, but men are limited in their reproductive capacity only by their access to women. In short, polygyny leads to greater reproductive success for men.

The polygyny threshold model helps explain why such systems perseverate independent of the sexual drives for diversity that may motivate many men to pursue them (and indeed may function as part of the natural selection pressure driving the evolution of such preferences). This model shows that rich women do a little better, but rich men do much better in terms of reproductive success by age sixty (Irons 1979). It is not trivial that wives of rich husbands do a little better in terms of reproductive success; this supplies part of the internal incentive for women to continue to participate in these practices. However, polygynous men benefit disproportionately because they can have many more children. They do not have more children per wife (necessarily), but they have many more wives who have children, and they can continue to replace older wives with younger ones who retain reproductive capacity as they themselves age. In other words, men use their power and wealth to achieve reproductive advantage and to gain status and wealth from other men by controlling access to women, who are the limiting factor in reproductive capacity because of long pregnancies.

The polygyny threshold model makes some important predictions. It predicts polygyny where there is large wealth inequality among men. Recall that where everyone is poor, ecologically imposed monogamy tends to rule. In other words, when there is no wealth discrepancy among men, monogamy becomes the default because it is (rightly) assumed that the vast majority of women prefer an unmarried male as a father. This is because women tend to benefit disproportionately from the pair bond in ways men do not. For example, in traditional societies where the father leaves or dies, children's survival rate declines by over 50 percent (Hill and Hurtado 1992). Whereas men may have many children, women tend to have fewer, and those children benefit from increased, and not divided, attention from their fathers.

However, this model also predicts that polygyny results in part as a result of female interests. Although there is little reproductive inequality among women, primarily because of biological limits, women do have slightly better reproductive success being married to a wealthier man. What this all leads to is an emphasis on the importance of male control of resources. Without it, men lose access not only to reproductive success for themselves, but also to the source of much of their own wealth and status. Wealth allows access to their own reproductive future but also allows them to generate wealth and status for themselves by maintaining control over the daughters that other men covet. Once such control weakens, as the prospect of female emancipation threatens, the entire social structure of their wealth and status becomes compromised, explaining why such men can, and do, fight to the death to retain such control.

The insight produced by understanding this dynamic leads to some important, perhaps inadvertent but critical consequences. For example, as Dickeman (1979) notes, the ecology of hypergyny, or females marrying up, encourages a stratification in societies whereby the wealthiest men buy the most women, women compete to be attractive to increase their odds of gaining a wealthy husband, and such men privilege easily guarded mates, since they have many distractions. This is not a new phenomenon. As Betzig (1993) writes, such tendencies have been common to powerful men across historical time in all major civilizations. In cultures and societies from Mesopotamia and the Ottoman Empire to Egypt, from the Aztec societies to India and China, powerful men sought to mate with hundreds if not thousands of women who were carefully secluded, guarded, often by eunuchs in large harems. Significantly, many eunuchs can and did have sex with women; they just could not reproduce, leaving no doubt about paternity under such circumstances. Rich, powerful men chose virgins, and terrible punishments for female adultery existed. In addition, powerful, wealthy men had open access to women of less powerful men, such as the iconic biblical story of David and Bathsheba illustrates. In addition, in many of these civilizations across time, many of these powerful men selected a single male heir and imposed celibacy on other younger sons and daughters in order to ensure lines of succession. The root of imposed suicide on widows can be located in such incentives as well. It is easy to assume that these perversions lay in the distant past, with no current reflections, but as our data show, such confidence fails to recognize the ghosts of such practices inhabiting the modern environment.

A Theoretical Link between Polygyny and Violence

The background provided above should help support a foundation for understanding the link between individual preferences in marriage and large-scale societal consequences. This is because polygyny, by virtue of the sex ratio imbalance described above, leaves a lot of men without wives. Unmarried men under age twenty-five tend to be disproportionately prone to violence because of higher levels of testosterone. First, age structure matters, and having a younger population tends to occur in places with highly fertile polygynous families. Second, men's testosterone declines precipitously in the two years surrounding marriage, and with the birth of each child, and rises again in the two years around divorce (Mazur and Booth 1998; Mazur and Michalek 1998; Gray et al. 2002). The joke is not that all the nice guys are married, but rather that guys are nice because they are married. Let me be absolutely clear here. It is not that testosterone itself causes violence; it is rather the case that testosterone makes men more likely to respond to challenges, particularly challenges to their status. Link this to the realization that it is the wealthy and powerful men who are more likely to be married, and one begins to see the problems that result from young, low-status men with few prospects having their status challenged. For one thing, the majority of murders are committed by unmarried men aged twenty to twenty-nine (Daly and Wilson 1999).

These dynamics produce economic, social, and political consequences that have been investigated in pieces in previous work. Economically, Michèle Tertilt conducted an analysis of twenty-two countries in sub-Saharan Africa and demonstrated that "banning polygyny decreases fertility by 40 percent, increases savings by 70 percent, and increases output per capita by 170 percent" (2005, 1341). In addition, children of polygynous unions were more than 24 percent more likely to die than were those born to monogamous families. Further, there are untold consequences from precipitating sexual activity on young girls, which frequently occurs in these societies where wealthy men prefer virgins, driving the age of marriage ever younger to ensure premarital chastity. Early sexual trauma leads to increased morbidity and a twenty-year increase in all-cause mortality (meaning death from any reason, not just related to the original trauma) regardless of the circumstances. Thus, as we document empirically, polygyny contributes to a decline in longevity. In addition, there is preliminary evidence that such trauma can also lead to the intergenerational transfer of changes in genetic expression, as occurred with increased diabetes risk in children born to Dutch women who gave birth during the terrible famine in 1943–44. In addition, children of young mothers have worse outcomes in education and long-term economic prospects, and higher risk for crime.

Valerie Hudson and Andrea den Boer (2004) carefully document many additional political consequences from sex ratio imbalance, such as those precipitated by polygynous practices. They demonstrate the important link between family structures and political outcomes. In particular, they show that sex ratio imbalance is associated with aggressive foreign policy initiatives as states seek to incentivize monastic or mercenary efforts in order to divert and distract young men from turning their rage on the state. Young men have their own individual incentives to engage in such battles and conquests. Historically, and apparently still in parts of central Asia, bride capture was a potential benefit of raiding, especially if someone was not able to find a wife at home. Indeed, the fairy tale of a prince charming on a white horse come to sweep a woman off her feet likely originated in such practices, since the typical central Asian horse is small and white. This story also shows how bad the lives of women were, that some preferred capture to continuing in their families of origins. In addition, men who engaged in such battle had the prospect of taking bounty or otherwise gaining status that would raise their likelihood of being able to afford a wife once they returned home. From the perspective of governments, if many of these young men were killed, that only helped the sex ratio imbalance. These strategies can take many forms. Current efforts on the part of the Chinese government to send students to the United States for graduate school can be understood in this light; of course, they want their students to learn English and obtain a Western education, but they also may want them to find first- or second-generation Chinese wives willing to return to China, since China currently suffers from one of the most extreme sex ratio imbalances in the world. Although their pattern results not from polygyny but rather from a one-child policy in the context of severe son preference, the consequences of such an imbalance at a societal level remain similar. In addition, Hudson and den Boer (2002) show that sex ratio imbalances are associated with repressive and authoritarian governments and uneven wealth distribution, as Betzig (1993) noted in her historical analysis of the consequences of polygyny. All these dynamics increase the propensity to violence.

Importantly, note that the processes I describe here are macrolevel outcomes that result not from individuals making long-term choices about large societal outcomes; instead, they emerge in a kind of hidden-hand fashion from the aggregation of individual incentives that privilege polygyny for the wealthy few, and yet produce mass dislocation and violence for the majority at a macro level. In this way, the story is not that different in structure from the one told about the top 1 percent of people who benefit from capitalist structures while many others suffer, yet nothing changes because power remains in the hands of the wealthy and powerful. In this area, the difference lies in the content and the significance of the exertion of this power by polygynous men on women.

The Investigation

Let me now return to my journey toward the study of polygyny. From the time of Wrangham's charge, it took about a decade to accumulate the data to test his hypotheses. But another odd 9/11 circumstance profoundly affected the direction of my search. I was scheduled to give a talk at Berkeley that required me to cross the country when the planes were not flying. So I took the train, which took about three and a half days each way. On the train, somewhere across the Midwest, I read a manuscript I had been sent to review by *International Security*. The manuscript absolutely blew me away. It turned out to be the "Bare Branches" piece written by Hudson and den Boer. Although I did not know who the authors were at the time, since the review was blind, I strongly endorsed the paper and said my name could be revealed to the authors—something I rarely do. Valerie Hudson contacted me, and we began a series of conversations about mutual interests. I told her about my project on polygyny, and she told me about the WomanStats Project she was just beginning. I joined as a principal investigator. Hudson's tireless and intrepid efforts with an army of diligent coders allowed us to collect the information I needed to conduct the analyses in the chapter devoted to the effect of polygyny on violence toward women and children and on the nation-state. All the data in that chapter derive from this database, which now contains data on over 270 variables for each of over 170 countries on a wide variety of laws and practices regarding women and children. All data are on the web, free to all, and we hope to encourage scholars to use this data set, which includes both qualitative and quantitative information, to analyze the many other facets of women and security that remain to be explored.

In addition, this work, and the robustness of these findings, inspired me to ask a question about attitudes toward polygyny in another unrelated study, in which I undertook experimental manipulations embedded in population samples that were nationally representative by gender and religion. We conducted these studies in Lebanon, Jordan, Uganda, Indonesia, and four regions in India, including Delhi. The Indian study was overseen by a remarkable graduate student I had at Brown, Michael Dickerson, who had lived in India for three years prior to graduate school and wrote his dissertation on patriarchal attitudes toward women in India. We asked questions across nine different areas in the larger study, but the chapter here concentrates exclusively on the question related to polygyny. That work constitutes a separate chapter in this volume, although both pieces are united in their focus on polygyny, with one investigating the sources of such behaviors by looking at individual attitudes and the other examining the consequences.

The Findings

As with any standard analysis, we were investigating the influence of an independent variable, in this case polygyny, on a series of dependent variables, which were the factors we thought polygyny might affect. For polygyny, after a decade of collecting data, I led a team through Woman-Stats to develop an overarching scale to code the degree of polygyny in any given country. The measure was a five-point scale from 0 to 4. A score of 0 was given where polygyny is illegal and rare, comprising less than 2 percent of marriages. A country received a 1 if polygyny was illegal and the law is enforced but multiple cohabitations exist that amount to more than 2 percent of the population; this typically occurs when there are certain ethnic or sectarian enclaves that practice polygyny within a larger society where monogamy remains the rule of law. A country scored 2 when polygyny is illegal except for specific exceptions for religious or ethnic minorities, and where less than 5 percent of women are in such marriages. A country received a 3 when polygyny was legal and less than 25 percent of women were in such marriages, and got a 4 when more than 25 percent of women were in such marriages.

In order to determine whether the effect of any given outcome was related to polygyny independent of the leading other explanatory variables, we also controlled for the wealth of a country, measured in gross domestic product in U.S. dollars. This is because, all else being equal, we would expect, and indeed we find, that, on average, women do better in wealthier countries. This should not be a surprise; when there are more resources, there is more to go around. However, it is absolutely crucial to recognize that many wealthy countries still show very high rates of violence against women in various forms, from domestic violence and rape to murder, as well as other negative outcomes. When the data were analyzed for the Canadian case, this ranged from the poorest country in the world at the time (Ethiopia at $120), to the richest country in the world (Luxembourg at $78,442).

A word of caution needs to be inserted here about the relationship between country wealth and data collection in general, but especially regarding issues related to women. Discrepancies in national wealth can make it difficult to calibrate data across countries because richer countries are more likely to care about, and spend money to collect, data on variables affecting women. So, in an odd perversion, it can look like Sweden is way worse on some measure of violence than, say, Nigeria simply because Sweden spends a lot of resources to record every case and collects accurate data whereas many poorer countries do not have the resources, and sometimes do not have the interest, to collect such data. So researchers need to be very careful about accepting at face value cross-cultural data, particularly regarding women. Such data can reflect a lot of deeply embedded cultural values, and they may not be an accurate reflection of what is really taking place on the ground. That is why, for example, WomanStats is careful to record both law and practice, because they often run in opposite directions, particularly in nondemocratic or poorer countries.

We also conducted a control for sex ratio, but because it did not prove statistically significant over and above the effects of polygyny in any of our analyses we did not include those analyses in the bulk of our presentations. The reason for this likely has to do with age structure, because sex ratio includes older women past reproductive age, and, on average, women live longer than men so there are more of them at older ages. However, the existence of these women would not be expected to drive the effects we examine here because they are past the reproductive age at which men compete for women, and this is the crucial factor that theoretically should drive the effects on violence we examine, for the reasons described above. Because these effects turned out as expected, there was no independent statistical effect for sex ratio, and because polygyny drove the findings, I will not say any more about that here except to note that we did control statistically for whether that factor alone was driving our effects.

We then examined the effect of polygyny on a large variety of dependent variables related to the health of women and children and the security and stability of the overall nation-state. This analysis involved every country in the world for which we were able to obtain data, a sample that constituted almost the entire universe of countries. This allowed us to compare the effects of low versus high levels of polygyny on various outcomes. And we looked at a lot of different outcomes. These included a WomanStats omnibus scale of women's physical security that incorporated rates of rape, murder, domestic violence, honor killings, and how strict the laws are for reporting and enforcing these crimes. We examined the effect on female genital mutilation, measured on a scale from 0 to 2 where 0 denotes virtually no women are subjected to such cutting and 2 coded in cases where more than half of women in that country are subjected to such practices. We also examined rates of sex trafficking, average age of marriage, birth rates, and female life expectancy. In addition, we looked at rates of maternal mortality measured in terms of deaths per one thousand live births. We also considered differences in the rates of male versus female HIV rates in a country. For factors affecting children, we looked at rates of both primary and secondary education for both boys and girls. Recall that polygyny benefits a minority of men, and hurts a majority of boys, who must be thrust out of the marriage market in order to sustain asymmetric access to women, so although it works out well for a minority of wealthy men, it hurts most boys and men.

We also examined several factors that affected domestic state–level stability and equality. Specifically, we looked at measures from WomanStats that ranked inequity in family law, which ranks the degree to which privilege in such things as inheritance, child custody, and divorce favors men over women. We also looked at discrepancy between law and practice that measures, for example, the extent to which there may be a law on the books that prohibits marriage before the age of sixteen or makes rape a crime, and yet these laws are rarely if ever enforced.

Finally, we looked at factors that may influence the international stability and security of a state. In this regard, we examined defense expenditures on weapons made by a country in a given year, as well as the degree of civil rights and political liberties enjoyed by the citizens of a particular country, using the standard measures from the political science literature, as documented in the technical chapter on these findings. It should be noted that the real outlier in this analysis is the United States simply because American weapons expenditures so far outweigh any other country on the globe.

The outcome is simple and can be summarized in very short form: higher rates of polygyny lead to much more negative outcomes for women, children, and nation-states across the board. As polygyny increases, the age of marriage for women declines, often well into childhood, while birth rates and rates of maternal mortality increase and overall life expectancy decreases. In short, polygyny costs a lot of women and children their lives.

The mechanism by which this occurs is enforced by biological exigencies: births to young mothers are much riskier, and short interbirth intervals, where children are born less than eighteen months apart, also raise risks for all kinds of maternal problems. Such births increase rates of birth defects as well. Although we were not able to obtain sufficient data to look at interbirth interval, other studies indicate that this declines in highly polygynous environments. As a result, when a girl is married very young—an outcome that benefits the father who wants the resources or alliance such a marriage entails, and the husband who increases his confidence of obtaining a disease-free virgin where his paternity rights are secure, as well as whatever intrinsic pleasure he may derive from having sex with a very young girl—she is less able to carry a healthy baby to term than say an eighteen- or twenty-year-old. She will likely be very fertile because of her age and so will get pregnant quickly after giving birth, having short interbirth intervals. Now some women may trade off productive and reproductive work by trading the timing of agricultural and childbirth responsibilities with other women in a family; however, that is only likely in environments where women work in agriculture, for example, and are not simply secluded by great wealth where such considerations would not come into play.

In addition to these effects on mortality itself, polygyny affects morbidity as well. As polygyny increases, rates of sex trafficking increase, rates of female genital mutilation increase, rates of domestic violence increase, and sex difference in HIV infection, such that many more women than men become infected, increases as well. Effects on children fare no better. Rates of both primary and secondary education decline for both girls and boys as rates of polygyny rise.

And the negative effects of polygyny are not restricted to the micro unit of the family. Rather, polygyny exerts profound and widespread societal impact as well. Specifically, as rates of polygyny rise, inequity in family law increases, as does discrepancy between law and practice. Even including the United States, which has relatively low rates of polygyny and huge amounts of weapons procurements, weapons spending increases overall as polygyny rises. Where polygyny rates are high, civil liberties decline, as do political rights. This makes sense because it requires a great deal of political, institutional, and cultural oppression to control the productive and reproductive capacity of half the population.

There are, of course, other factors that may be associated with polygyny that we were not able to explore. For example, we did not have sufficient coverage across countries on rates of prostitution or pornography to examine the effect of polygyny on these outcomes. While it is certainly theoretically possible that there are some positive features associated with polygyny, all of the cases we have heard remain anecdotal in nature. We were not able to find a single one that could be supported at an aggregate level statistically. Jonathan Cowden did an incredibly meticulous and diligent analysis of all these data in both empirical pieces in this volume (chapters 3 and 4).

The findings are clear, consistent, and statistically robust across the board. In fact, the results are the kind of thing most social scientists strive for but almost never find in the course of their careers. If these findings were about something not related to women, chances are that they would be treated as revolutionary in international relations theory; indeed, the effects are much stronger than those supporting the notion of the democratic peace that has spawned an entire cottage industry of inquiry. I leave it to the reader to ponder why powerful effects regarding the treatment of women on the health and security of states do not receive such extensive attention.

Canadian Trial

Sometimes, however, real life does pay attention to scholarly efforts. One day, I was sitting in my office at the University of California, Santa Barbara, when I got a call out of the blue from Joanne Klineberg, from the Canadian Attorney General's Office. She told me about the polygamy reference case they were working on, for which they needed someone who had statistical data on polygyny. She asked me if I might consider working as an expert witness for them on this case. I had never worked in such a capacity before, but the topic had by then become very important to me; I had become convinced by my data of the harm done by polygyny. By this time, I had done a lot of work on polygyny, so I agreed.

The trial took place in Vancouver near Christmas in 2010, and it was a truly fascinating experience for me. In Canada, the laws are somewhat different from those of the United States, so standing is not necessary to bring suit; reference trials can take place adjudicating the constitutionality of a law without someone experiencing harm as a result of it. I learned a great deal from the incredibly diligent team working in the Attorney General's Office in British Columbia, which included B. J. Wray. The team helped prepare me for my testimony and supported me throughout my experience. The most amazing thing to me about this trial is that the majority of the expert witnesses for the other side made points that were entirely consistent with my own analysis, making me wonder why they had been called. I testified for parts of a couple of different days and presented the data, analysis, and graphs that appear in chapter 3. I explained the work I had done and the findings that came out of the analysis. The opposing side that cross-examined me had some strategies to try to unnerve and distract me in the courtroom, but none came close to being as disturbing as teaching a large class of undergraduates glued to their iPhones, so I found none of it problematic.

The trial was stopped for a period shortly after my testimony when the Canadian Royal Mounties indeed found and stopped an incidence of sex trafficking. They discovered that several young girls were being sent from the Bountiful community of Fundamentalist Latter Day Saints to a related group across the border in Utah, demonstrating in a very real way one of the effects about which I had just testified.

The judge was, in my opinion, a serious and thoughtful person trying hard to weigh the relative merit of arguments that rested primarily on the importance of freedom of religion on the one hand and the documented negative consequences of polygyny on the other. He took almost a year to render his decision, which was not surprising given that the material the case generated took up the entirety of a small room. In the end, he sided with upholding the constitutional prohibition of polygamy, the side for which I had advocated. In his judgment, Chief Justice Robert Bauman wrote: "I find that Dr. McDermott's report was conducted on the basis of well-proven methodology and utilized data of unparalleled scope and quality. Her scientific method and the results it produced cannot be dismissed on the basis of what can only be characterized as a lay person's appeal to so-called common sense. Dr. McDermott's analysis does prove 'something.' As she says in the conclusion to her report (at para. 158) 'polygyny's negative effects are wide-ranging, statistically demonstrated, and independently verified using alternative analytical tools.' I find Dr. McDermott's evidence to be compelling" (at para. 640).

I had not realized how influential this decision was for other areas of Canadian law until several years later when I was teaching a graduate seminar. There was a Canadian political theory student in the class, and for some reason the discussion veered into freedom of religion. He then started talking about legal restrictions on freedom of religion akin to those on free speech that prevent people from falsely screaming fire in a crowded theater. The case started to sound eerily familiar until I realized he was talking about the polygamy reference trial. I said, "Oh, I was the expert witness in that trial." His eyes bugged out of his head, he dropped his pen, and he blurted out, "Oh my God, that was you! *You* are the harm person." I was shocked and asked him what he meant, thinking he was accusing me of causing harm to the whole of Canada. He then proceeded to explain that the larger implication of the case was that it supported circumscribing freedom of religion in cases where such liberty could render undue harm on individuals because the state had a substantial interest in preventing such harm. Obviously, the overarching principle here may remain controversial, but I agree that this decision weighs on the right side of both law and virtue.

I was extremely proud of this work. It was one of the few times in my life where I felt the academic work I had done had achieved an important real-world outcome and might have helped, however marginally, to improve the lives of some people over time. It was an extremely gratifying feeling.

Experimental Study

Once the widespread and negative consequences of polygyny were clear, the next obvious step was to embark on a process of trying to discover and uncover some of the underlying causes of these practices. This is not such an easy step because the prevalence of polygyny differs quite a bit around the globe, and complex social and political phenomena often result from multiple causes, any one of which can be sufficient to produce the effect under observation. But examining how attitudes vary depending on the determinative demographic circumstances of a person's life seems a reasonable place to start, and so that is how the second empirical study in this volume came to be.

When I embarked on a project designed to examine the nature of attitudes toward sexual inequality in various countries around the world, I realized this project offered an opportunity to explore some of the potential sources of attitudes toward polygyny in that context. The larger study is an embedded experiment, meaning that an experimental manipulation is embedded in a nationally representative sample. For many of the questions regarding other topics, like health and education, the manipulation asks some individuals to make the decision about their daughter and others about their son; they are not aware that different people get different versions of the question, and thus we can traction the differences between respondents to examine the effect of sex on their attitudes in certain domains. In the case of the polygyny question, we made it a bit more complicated, asking people if a man who wants to take a second wife should do so, where in one case his first wife approves and in the other case she objects. In our study, the samples were representative by sex and religion, meaning the population we examined accurately reflected the overall percentages of those groups in the broader society. This strategy allows us to statistically examine the influence of the sex and religion of the subjects to determine whether those variables have an effect on people's attitudes. This design allows us to gain both control and validity in our study.

In this examination, which appears in chapter 4, we surveyed about 1,200 in each of several countries including Lebanon, Jordan, Uganda, Indonesia, and several provinces of India (Bihar, Punjab, Kerala, and Delhi) to include over ten thousand respondents. This large grouping allowed us to examine the effect of sex and religion as potential sources in creating underlying attitudes toward polygyny. We found that religion did not have as much of an influence as people might have thought but, not surprisingly, sex does have an effect, with women in general much less likely to support polygyny than men regardless of the condition.

Policy Implications

I understand I was chosen as the first Easton Lecturer in part because my work does not fit into traditional frameworks or paradigms. It challenges existing or traditional wisdom, something Easton's work also did. The work on polygyny certainly falls into that category. Indeed, I have never conducted any work in my career that has aroused such consistent, extreme, and visceral opposition. Ironically much of this indignation emanates from so-called feminists in particular. In my experience, many of them dismiss my data without presenting anything more substantial than anecdotes on the other sides of the equation. Much of this misguided feminist criticism originated in political correctness, a misdirected attempt to respect cultural diversity without recognition of the consequences of such respect for protecting basic human rights, human dignity, and female health and welfare. The opposition rests mostly on arguments that privilege personal choice and freedom. Of course we know examples of people who happily reside in polyamorous households in the United States or other Western, industrialized developed countries. But such an environment offers great diversity and opportunity for choice, where women in such circumstances have, in Hirschman's (1970) terms, both voice as well as the ability to exit situations that no longer work for them. This is very different from the kinds of circumstances or environments in which most women in polygynous marriages around the globe exist. Such women have no voice, and no opportunity for exit, since they are wholly socially and financially dependent on the men in their lives because they are consistently denied education and financial independence. Such a situation could not be more different from that of a bisexual woman in Cambridge with a PhD, making a couple of hundred thousand dollars a year, who decides to live with both her male and female lovers. Those privileged women should not assume that their lives and choices reflect in any way whatsoever the circumstances of violence and oppression that characterize the lives of their poor, uneducated sisters throughout the world. Many privileged women focus on notions of personal freedom both because they do not fully understand the kinds of circumstances endured by most women in polygynous marriages around the world and also because they themselves consider choice so important in their own lives, as indeed it is. But if we think of this in terms of Maslow's (1971) hierarchy of needs, women whose basic needs are met have the luxury to focus on issues of personal choice and freedom, whereas women whose basic health and safety is at risk do not. This is what many people who focus on choice fail to fully accept. None of these privileged women would want to live a life of fear and deprivation, as the vast majority of women around the world do, but they are not forced to do so. Yet their polygynous sisters do not have a similar choice to leave their lives for alternative ones of privilege. While a position privileging personal choice and freedom may easily make sense in wealthy, educated populations where women have independent resources and can exit situations not to their liking, this is not the reality in the vast majority of polygynous unions around the globe where women are given or sold in marriages before they reach the age of majority and remain financially and socially dependent on men who may abuse them. In such circumstances, notions of personal choice and freedom remain little more than chimeras. For example, in the Canadian trial, I heard personal testimony from people who said that naked baby girls would be held under freezing cold running water until they stopped crying in order to get them to keep quiet. Anyone who knows anything about normal, healthy child development realizes that these are precisely the conditions that would make a normal child cry. It would take a lot for a child to learn to be quiet in this torturous situation, but likely only one trial learning to never make noise again so as to avoid such horrible abuse. If such children are conditioned by such abuse to be quiet and submissive prior to the time they even develop language, then we can hardly expect them as they grow older to challenge their fathers and husbands in the same way that a highly educated woman from a healthy family of origin would be expected to do. These abused women most often lack the education, resources, or wherewithal to leave circumstances of oppression and abuse should they wish to do so. They would have nowhere to go, no one to turn to, and no resources to support them. Further, many of the areas where such practices are endemic lack the variety of state and private safe houses that exist in much of the industrialized world. Such circumstances limit rather than enhance prospects for personal freedom and security.

The second point of opposition usually rests on arguments about respect for cross-cultural differences in norms and values. This certainly constitutes a valid point, but here is where reasonable people can disagree, and I tend to side with the Canadian chief justice. When such practices cause demonstrable harm, then such practices are not neutral in their effects. It is not only justifiable but also incumbent on those who claim to value the lives of women to speak out against these practices. Support for such practices serves only to perpetuate the patterns of abuse and violence they engender and support. In this regard, I was particularly struck by B. J. Wray's insight that in order to produce a result that might protect women against all these negative outcomes, the government would have to enact at least eighteen different laws to produce the same positive effect that outlawing polygyny has. To me, that recognition encompassed everything meaningful regarding the profound and pervasive negative impact of polygyny on women, children, and the security, freedom, and stability of a state.

This is not to say that polygyny is the only, or even the single most important, cause of violence or other kinds of political pathology or domestic calamity. Many social structures harm women and children and help precipitate violence; unfortunately, the sources of such violence result from multiple sufficient causation. Viewed from this perspective, polygyny constitutes a sufficient but not necessary cause of the many kinds of harm detailed throughout this volume. In this way, polygyny represents one potential cause of many, enough on its own to cause the systematic, diverse, and myriad negative consequences noted here; however, there are unfortunately many other structural factors that alone and in combination can precipitate similar widespread damage. These factors range from cultural biases, such as patriarchy, through to normative constraints, which include the existence of laws that either permit or encourage systematic discrimination against women, most notably in the area of family and reproductive law. Along with polygyny, some of the most important structural factors contributing to widespread and systematic bias against women include, but are not limited to, patrilocality (Hudson et al. 2008/9; Hudson, Bowen, and Nielsen 2015), sex ratio imbalance (Hudson and den Boer 2002, 2004), and disproportionately high bride price through most of the non-Western world (Hudson and Matfess 2017).

So what are the broader policy implications of these findings? At least several important ramifications are worthy of consideration. First, these findings suggest that conventional female empowerment techniques, such as education alone, may not work to free women from male social and economic control in many parts of the world. It is not that literacy does not matter, nor should efforts to increase literacy be halted. But it is also important to recognize that reading material can often be controlled by men, and so literacy in isolation may not necessarily increase female empowerment or financial independence. In fact, under many circumstances, women's challenging their husbands or fathers may lead to increased violence being directed at them, at least in the short run.

Second, small business loans to women may increase their financial independence and prospects for their children's education, especially girls' education. But again, there is some suggestive evidence from places like India that as the household gets richer, men prevent their wives from working, since having a wife who does not work gives them status with other men. This then serves further to isolate and restrict the freedom of movement of many of these women. So again, loans alone may help, but loans may not prove the panacea to development woes many hope they will provide.

Finally, it can be very difficult to advocate for Western values such as monogamy when such efforts may simply appear as implicit latter-day forms of colonial oppression, imposing foreign values on countries that do not espouse them. However, it is important to recognize the importance of restricting polygynous practices if we truly want to improve basic human rights, such as health, and mitigate the injustice that follows from deep forms of gender inequality. It may be that such efforts must emanate from within cultures that embrace these practices, and such efforts may begin with the men who are deprived of wives altogether or as a secondary consequence of objections to tremendous inequality in overall wealth.

I never would have guessed that a project begun so casually in response to a question from a respected mentor would lead to such a long and robust research path, although admittedly that is not the first time something like that has happened. I have learned a great deal along the way and have been blessed by some amazing and committed collaborators. I must say that my data have depressed me. They have made me, if possible, more cynical than I already was about human nature and our capacity to be kind or generous toward one another. But this project has also convinced me more than ever that if we want to change the world, we must begin by changing ourselves. Huge problems—such as terrorism and economic dislocation and violence—do not happen in isolation. Nor do they come out of nowhere. Rather, they result from children's experiencing and witnessing violence and hatred in their lives and coming to believe that such actions are appropriate mechanisms of conflict resolution. Children listen, and they learn from what they see around them. Why should we be surprised that children come to believe that might equals right because that is the relationship they see between their mothers and father? Children do not outgrow such developmental disturbances. Instead, they carry such a paradigm of inequality and violence into their larger personal, professional, and social lives and seek to re-create hierarchies of dominance that are natural, but also learned. The importance of incorporating such factors, which are too often overlooked or ignored, into any comprehensive analysis of large-scale societal problems constitutes the next chapter of this volume, coauthored with Peter K. Hatemi.

We can analyze ISIS and similar and past extremist groups in terms of radical religious beliefs all we want, and that indeed may tell part of the story. But it does not tell the entire story. The fact that such groups recruit and use sex slaves and seek to enslave women under their charge is not accidental. It is part of their philosophy and purpose. Polygyny promotes weaker and more superficial marital bonds by its very nature, if only because of limited attention and distraction. As long as the bond between husband and wife is weak relative to the bond between mother and son, then violence against women will promulgate at higher rates. Of course patrilocality exacerbates this effect, because under such conditions, a woman's safety from other men can be assured only by the loyalty of her son's protection, since she no longer has access to her father or brothers for safety and succor. All these processes sit on a fundamental foundation of male coalitionary psychology that privileges group cohesion over dyadic engagement, contrary to female psychology, which tends to privilege pair bonds. Yet while male and female reproductive drives, and the psychological processes such instincts entrain, often do not fit very well with each other, both sides want to raise their children successfully, on average. This is the place where rational and emotional interest can coalesce and intervene to encourage parents to join in reducing the intergenerational transmission of the kind of gender-based violence that compromises the prospects for peace in the future for all of us.

References

Betzig, Laura. 1993. "Where Are the Bastards' Daddies?" *Behavioral and Brain Sciences* 16:284–85.

Daly, Martin, and Margo Wilson. 1999. "Darwinism and the Roots of Machismo." *Scientific American* 10:8–14.

Dickeman, Mildred. 1979. "Comment on van den Berghe's and Barash's Sociobiology." *American Anthropologist* 81:351–57.

Gray, J. Patrick. 1998. "*Ethnographic Atlas Codebook* Derived from George P. Murdock's *Ethnographic Atlas* Recording the Marital Composition of 1231 Societies from 1960 to 1980." *World Cultures* 10 (1): 86–136.

Gray, Peter B., Sonya M. Kahlenberg, Emily S. Barrett, Susan F. Lipson, and Peter T. Ellison. 2002. "Marriage and Fatherhood Are Associated with Lower Testosterone in Males." *Evolution and Human Behavior* 23 (3): 193–201.

Hirschman, Albert O. 1970. *Exit, Voice, and Loyalty: Responses to Decline in Firms, Organizations, and States.* Cambridge, MA: Harvard University Press.

Hudson, Valerie M., and Hilary Matfess. 2017. "In Plain Sight: The Neglected Linkage between Brideprice and Violent Conflict." *International Security* 42 (1): 7–40.

Hudson, Valerie M., Donna Lee Bowen, and Perpetua Lynne Nielsen. 2015. "Clan Governance and State Stability: The Relationship between Female Subordination and Political Order." *American Political Science Review* 109:535–55.

Hudson, Valerie M., Mary Caprioli, Bonnie Ballif-Spanvill, Rose McDermott, and Chad F. Emmett. 2008/9. "The Heart of the Matter: The Security of Women and the Security of States." *International Security* 33 (3): 7–45.

Hudson, Valerie M., and Andrea M. den Boer. 2002. "A Surplus of Men, a Deficit of Peace: Security and Sex Ratios in Asia's Largest States." *International Security* 26 (4): 5–38.

———. 2004. *Bare Branches: The Security Implications of Asia's Surplus Male Population.* Cambridge, MA: MIT Press.

Hurtado, A. M., and K. R. Hill. 1992. "Paternal Effect on Offspring Survivorship among Ache and Hiwi Hunter-Gatherers: Implications for Modeling Pair-Bond Stability." *Father-Child Relations: Cultural and Biosocial Contexts*, edited by Barry S. Hewlett, 31–55. New York: de Gruyter.

Irons, William. 1979. "Cultural and Biological Success." In *Evolutionary Biology and Human Social Behavior: An Anthropological Perspective*, edited by Napoleon A. Chagnon and William Irons, 284–302. North Scituate, MA: Duxbury Press.

Maslow, Abraham H. 1971. *The Farther Reaches of Human Nature.* New York: Viking.

Mazur, Allan, and Alan Booth. 1998. "Testosterone and Dominance in Men." *Behavioral and Brain Sciences* 21:353–63.

Mazur, Allan, and Joel Michalek. 1998. "Marriage, Divorce and Male Testosterone." *Social Forces* 77:315–30.

Tertilt, Michèle. 2005. "Polygyny, Fertility, and Savings." *Journal of Political Economy* 113 (6): 1341–71.

Van den Berghe, Pierre L. 1987. *The Ethnic Phenomenon.* New York: Praeger.

2

MAKING NEW GARMENTS FROM OLD CLOTH

Reincorporating Clinical and Developmental Psychology into Models of Political Behavior

Rose McDermott and Peter K. Hatemi

This chapter explains the why and the how of the methodology we used to explore this topic of polygyny. In reaching back to a venerable tradition in clinical and developmental research in psychology, we honor David Easton's concern with methodology and his interest in how our substantive findings and view of a body of knowledge are shaped by the approach to scientific inquiry that we follow. In short, the answers we discover are largely shaped by the kinds of questions we ask, and those questions are in turn formulated by the types of methods we employ to examine our issues of concern. We wanted to explicate this tradition in detail here to help illuminate why we examine the questions we do the way we do in subsequent chapters.

Many of the early and important developments in political-attitude research and survey methodology emerged from work that incorporated theories and methods derived from clinical and developmental psychology. However, as behaviorist and rational choice approaches emerged, the study of political behavior largely abandoned developmental and clinical psychology approaches. We seek here not only to describe and display the importance of this earlier work, and the critical contributions these areas generated for the study of political behavior in general and public opinion research in particular, but also to explicitly encourage the reincorporation of older models in developmental and clinical psychology into the study of political behavior. Although some recent investigations into the origins of political behaviors and preferences have begun to broaden by integrating new approaches from a variety of areas, including behavior genetics and cognitive neuroscience, with developmental and clinical models, many scholars remain unaware of the historical development or significance of these models and their relevance for the modern study of political attitudes, preferences, and behaviors. These approaches are newly poised to provide useful models and insights to inform our understanding of the nature of political behavior in more comprehensive and accurate ways.

We begin by tracing the history of developmental and clinical models of psychology in the study of political behavior, highlighting the importance of their contribution for the study of political behavior both historically and currently. Our goal here echoes the calls put forth by the National Institutes of Health (2011) for the interdisciplinary integration of fields in pursuit of novel resolutions to important social and political challenges, from public health to civic engagement. Publically available data sets, including the Adolescent Health panel studies (AddHealth), and funding mechanisms, such as OppNet, are designed to integrate the study of social systems and the nature of behavior. As such, they offer new opportunities for scholars to leverage historic clinical and developmental models to explore critical current political questions and problems. We begin by discussing some of the historical uses of developmental and clinical models in the study of political behavior and then proceed to discuss potential applications in each area independently.

Historical Developments

In many ways, developmental and clinical approaches provided many of the original foundations for current models in political behavior and political psychology writ large. Indeed, in earlier incarnations, psychologists investigating leaders often drew upon theories and themes in clinical psychology to try to help make sense of the decisions leaders made. For example, Lasswell's (1930) original work on leadership, *Psychopathology and Politics*, invoked the Freudian notion of projection to analyze the way in which leaders projected their internal needs and conflicts onto the political world. In addition, Alexander George and Juliet George's (1956) classic work on leadership, *Woodrow Wilson and Colonel House*, explicitly adopted a psychoanalytic approach in examining the repetition compulsion that defined Woodrow Wilson's noncompensatory psychological strategy. The Georges demonstrated how Wilson repeatedly handled powerful male authority figures with whom he came in conflict in a way that derived from his relationship with his father, illustrating the pattern with examples from the conflicts Wilson had with Dean West when he was president of Princeton University through his ultimately tragic fight with Senator Henry Cabot Lodge over the League of Nations at the end of the First World War. However, many of these leadership studies, largely restricted to more idiosyncratic case studies, faltered on the basis of their small sample size and inability to replicate or generalize widely across individuals. As the field grew and developed, this limitation gave way to increased focus on models being developed from then-recent developments in social psychology. This theoretical move coincided with the behavioral revolution in political science taking shape at places like the University of Chicago, with its greater emphasis on empirical rigor and replicability.

The incorporation of developmental psychology into the study of political behavior has a long history as well, although its current manifestation is often not recognized to derive from models in developmental psychology. However, all of attitudinal survey research, including that which constitutes the basis for public opinion polling and American National Election Studies, was founded on the methodological advances of behaviorism, which primarily rests on psychological social learning theory. For example, early work in voting studies conducted by Lazarsfeld and colleagues (Lipset et al. 1954; Lazarsfeld et al. 1968) investigating applied social research took advantage of methodological advances in survey research during the behavioral revolution pioneered by sociologists. This kind of behavioral research became largely incorporated into mainstream political science, albeit without widespread recognition of its origin in psychology. Indeed, the study of attitudes and attitudinal structure, unlike the work on leadership, survived in the face of the behavioral revolution precisely because political science proved able to develop theories of attitude development, change, and structure that were not rooted solely in psychological models in general or psychodynamic theory in particular, which came under increased criticism for lack of empirical support and theoretical underspecification.

As psychoanalytic theory collapsed as the dominant theory of human behavior in the wake of the behavioral revolution writ large, the study of attitudes, action, and behavior did not fall away in political science in the same way that leadership studies had, precisely because of the former's incorporation of behavioral methods into voting research. In the wake of this shift in emphasis, important and valuable new work in the study of political behavior emerged. For example, work epitomized by the so-called Michigan approach displaced purely behavioral models with a more psychological and attitudinal approach to voting. The most notable and influential work in this regard quickly became a classic. *The American Voter* (Campbell et al. 1960) employed nationwide surveys of large samples to uncover the dynamics underlying public opinion and American voting behavior. This argument located the source of political attitudes and behavior in an individual's psychological attachment to their political party, which was assumed to be learned at the knees of a parent. The notion here implicitly assumed a process of socialization whereby the parent's attachment to political party would be transferred to the child, whose attachment to the parent would potentiate an overlapping political identification. Such a model posited implicit social processes of group identification but failed to specify the particular psychological mechanisms by which these attachments developed. However, as political science moved into a more behavioral research tradition, the field largely abandoned its previous integration of other subfields within psychology and thus failed to interrogate the basis of such intergenerational transfer of political party identification. Ironically, this led to the near exclusion of the developmental and clinical traditions that had generated the very models that helped the field survive in the face of the behavioral revolution and that had earlier offered important contributions to our understanding of political leadership in particular.

Those political science departments that invested in psychology focused on early models of social psychology, and the few programs that did staff their departments with psychologists did not include developmental and clinical psychologists. As a result, the discipline of political science has remained largely alienated from modern work in developmental psychology and clinical psychiatry while these fields made advances in both methods and theory that redressed earlier limitations and offered potential broader applications in these areas.

Today, the majority of psychological models in political science depend primarily on insights largely drawn from models in early social psychology for applications and insights into the nature and foundations of political attitudes and behavior. Yet modern psychology has grown substantially as a discipline in ways not fully appreciated within the study of political behavior in political science. The rich resources offered by a full recognition of the historical significance and import of developmental and clinical psychology has been largely lost in the investigation of political attitudes, preferences, and behavior. Yet the modern instantiation of such models and arguments remains informative and relevant for many areas of interest in political science.

This use of psychology to study politics found adherents among those who, like Solomon Asch (1955) and Stanley Milgram (1974) in social psychology, shared an interest in trying to understand the motivation of Nazi Germany in general, and Hitler in particular, in perpetuating the genocide of Jews in Germany. Some of the early work in psychology, such as the largely discredited model put forward by Erikson (1968), drew on insights from psychodynamic models to explain the origin of Hitler's behavior. Other work with mass publics, undertaken using survey methods, such as work on the *Authoritarian Personality* by Adorno et al. (1950), explained the outcome in terms of more widespread societal anti-Semitism. This work came under intense methodological criticism by many who argued that the F-scale, designed to measure such attitudes, was constructed in a biased fashion (Brown 1986). More recent attempts to capture these beliefs and tie them to systematic political preferences and behavior, without falling prey to such methodological faults, come under the rubric of *Right-Wing Authoritarianism* (Altemeyer 1981). Classic work in social psychology, such as the work on conformity (Asch 1950) and obedience (Milgram 1974), proved their value by providing important situational motives for behavior that seemed otherwise incomprehensible. Theories developed in social psychology, employing sophisticated experimental designs, thus showed how ordinary people could engage in the banality of evil (Arendt 1963) without relying on deep psychological dysfunction or particular political belief structures.

Because such models proved so useful and insightful in the influence of groups (Moscovici 1985; Nemeth 1986) and the critical role of situations in influencing outcomes of interest (Zimbardo 2007) among many other topics, the developing field of political psychology continued to depend on the findings provided by this subfield to the relative neglect of developmental and clinical approaches. This resulted in no small part from the ways in which these approaches remained commensurate with, and reliant upon, the increased use of the survey and statistical analyses noted above. Because the dominant models of social psychology during this time emphasized the critical role of situation and environments on social behavior, and because such social behavior could be easily and readily ascertained through the survey method, the marriage between social and political psychology appeared made in heaven. However, this union served to re-create others in its own image and failed to support progeny whose outlook differed drastically either in ontological origin or methodological perspective. As political science becomes more integrated with the research findings generated in other fields, including behavioral economics, neuropsychology, genetics, and neurobiology, it becomes increasingly useful, if not necessary, to draw upon the insights generated by clinical and developmental psychology to improve the descriptive accuracy of models of human behavior. This perspective allows for the incorporation of a broader range of psychological models to more fully and accurately enlighten the enduring and important questions that motivate the study of political preferences.

This is important because clinical and developmental approaches have grown substantially in ways that are not fully appreciated within current models of political behavior, but are crucial for explicating neurobiological approaches that are becoming increasingly common in the field. Developmental and clinical models offer important perspectives for exploring the interplay between the development of individual minds and the social world, including explorations of the interactions between personality, emotion, prejudice and stereotyping, cooperation and aggression, identity and the self, attitudes and persuasion, and issues of perception and interpretation that influence our understanding of the political world.

Methodologically, they offer innovations that allow for the incorporation of extreme forms of behavior as well as those that lie within the normal range. These psychological models address these important and prominent concerns by incorporating models of neural and social development from fetus to adulthood and capturing all those life events, experiences, and biological mechanisms that lead to preferences, perception, values, and goals in many domains. Such forces guide behavior across domains and inevitably influence political choice. Clinical and developmental approaches today rely on a full complement of experimental, social, familial, longitudinal, and neurobiological methods. The modern instantiation of such models and arguments remains informative and relevant not only for cataloguing and explicating behaviors, but also for inspiring action to remediate suffering in more effective ways. Such a critical mission has been dissipating from the study of political behavior over the last several decades but continues to be championed by larger psychological science.

Clinical Psychology and Psychiatry

Clinical psychology encompasses a series of methods that have traditionally focused on diagnosis of behavior outside the normal range. This is not so different an approach from that favored in areas of political science that have also focused on extreme cases, such as war. There are numerous clinical methods that may be of use for the study of political traits. Here we concentrate on the study of extreme behavior because its understanding remains central. In clinical work, such efforts are devoted to attempts to alleviate immediate suffering, as well as providing insight into lesser versions of the same phenomena in the normal population. In a similar manner, political psychology can use such an approach to understand how extreme cases of particular phenomena, for example fear, might inform our understanding of how its manipulation in lesser form can influence political preferences in decisive ways.

Models and methods drawn from clinical psychology, which focus on understanding, preventing, and relieving psychological distress or dysfunction, have led to a deep understanding of critical core processes underlying human behaviors such as emotion, anxiety, fear, and affiliation. Clinical psychology and psychiatry hold great promise for helping political psychologists address the explicitly political implications of these emotions and associations. In particular, clinical approaches identify a condition and then seek to understand extreme manifestations in order to more fully explicate the mechanisms behind the condition and the resulting consequences if left untreated. Identification remains similarly useful for understanding the mechanisms and development of political behavior as well; isolating extreme exemplars of any given phenomenon helps observers to identify the processes by which biology and environment interact to create the expression of a particular thought, feeling, or behavior in a given context. Examining the sources of such variables at the extremes of a distribution helps us grasp the emergence of these forces within a more normal range. At the very least, investigating specific factors in their purest form can help guide, shape, and generate hypotheses concerning how they might operate in less pronounced form in different populations.

One of the premier forefathers of the combination of clinical psychology and political behaviors was the late Hans Eysenck. His work on intelligence and personality set the foundation for much of what we know of each today. Eysenck (1947, 1990) introduced the world to the two basic personality dimensions he theorized, extroversion and neuroticism, both of which he proposed as inherited and genetically influenced. Some sixty years later, countless theories and measures of personality have since emerged, using a variety of measures and scales, the best known of which is the five-factor model or so-called Big Five personality measure, often credited to Costa and McCrae (1985). This approach continues to recognize extroversion and neuroticism as two core components of personality, though not the only two, as Eysenck believed. The last thirty years of research in personality have validated Eysenck's initial finding that personality is related to biological and physiological individual dispositions (Bouchard et al. 1990; Bouchard and McGue 2003). The major importance of Eysenck's theories as they relate to political psychology lies in the clinical nature of his early identification of personality traits. His measurement instruments and questions were originally developed through observation of individuals who were either clinically neurotic or, alternatively, overly dependent on increased activity, social engagement, and other stimulation-seeking behaviors (extroverted). The questions on his clinically developed scale were then refined and subjected to the method of factor analysis, to produce one of the first combinations of a clinically developed and empirically validated measure of personality (Eysenck 1947), which he then applied to the study of politics (Eysenck 1954).

The works of Adorno et al. (1950), Eysenck (1954), Eysenck and Wilson (1978), Wilson (1973), and Wilson and Patterson (1968) set the stage for the research on personality and politics that has recently reemerged today. Earlier works in political science engaged this literature (McClosky and Bann 1979), but the study of personality and political preferences quieted at the same time that B. F. Skinner's behaviorist models and Milgram's social psychology models grew. However, the ideas spawned by Eysenck and his contemporaries have resurfaced in arguments surrounding the importance of clinical methods in exploring social traits. Much of the work that leading personality and politics scholars such as John Jost (Jost et al. 2003) and other contemporaries have produced regarding the relationship between personality and political attitudes constitutes, in many ways, a modern reenvisioning of work originally conducted by psychologists from the 1950s to the 1970s. Eysenck explored the relationship between ideology, attitudes, and personality (Eysenck 1954), the genetic nature of personality (Eysenck 1990), and even the genetic relationship between personality and attitudes (Eaves and Eysenck 1974). A half century later, the vast majority of contemporary research examining the relationship between personality and political attitudes is still being presented in psychology journals (Jost et al. 2003), even by political scientists (Bizer et al. 2004; Verhulst, Hatemi, and Martin 2010). When such work has been published in political science journals, it is more often authored by psychologists (Caprara et al. 2006; Carney et al. 2008). Recent trends demonstrate renewed interest in the relationship between personality and attitudes by political scientists within the political science literature, yet these works remain almost agnostic, if not completely unaware of, the clinical and theoretical origins and aspects of the measures (Mondak et al. 2010; Gerber et al. 2010).

Unfortunately, outside of research in personality, modern clinical approaches within political science have virtually disappeared, even for those traits that have major clinical importance. For example, the influence of fear poses a major research agenda for political behavior (Brader 2005; Jost et al. 2007). Certainly fear has been tied to ideology in the extant literature (Jost et al. 2008). However, the examination of individual levels of fear dispositions, along with the clinical nature of anxieties and phobias, has remained largely absent in the political behavior literature. Indeed, critical information on how fears are developed and maintained remains all but absent in political attitude research.

Yet clinical approaches have focused on diagnosing and treating fears and phobias and provide valuable information on how political behaviors may or may not be influenced by fear that varies by individual disposition. For example, Ainsworth and Bowlby (1991) identified innate fear dispositions based on infant reactions to unfamiliarity; Antony et al. (2005) found that adults with a higher degree of fear confronting novel social situations are less likely to compare themselves favorably to unfamiliar others; and Kendler et al. (1992) identified genetic influence on fears and phobias. In combination, these findings contribute interwoven strands into the weave of a larger literature that collectively agrees on the innate determinants of differential underlying fear dispositions (Balter 2010) that become socially modified and directed. Such findings are critically important for the study of political attitudes, preferences, and behavior, yet have not been integrated into their study in any systematic way. A great deal of work has been dedicated to identifying how fear motivates individuals to act in certain ways and how it can shift attitudes and vote choice. Additional research has examined how certain fear stimuli can mobilize the public toward a particular candidate or platform. Yet almost no research in this area has attempted to understand the source of such fears, or sought ways to extinguish it in order to protect the greater public from fear-based political rhetoric. In other words, almost no work has yet recognized the critical innate differences in baseline fear that have been already identified in clinical research (for an exception, see Hatemi et al. 2013).

Importantly, much clinical work has focused on extinguishing fear (Phelps and Thomas 2003; Schiller et al. 2010); such an agenda clearly fits well within the original mission of contributing to the public good espoused by political psychology. Indeed, a wide array of phobias and fears exist, but, as with cancer, one treatment does not fit all types. Social phobias are the most difficult to treat, and rarely if ever are cured, while animal and situational phobias are much more amenable to effective treatment. The partially innate and rigid nature of social fear has profound implications for political behaviors, because political institutions, attitudes, and preferences are profoundly social in nature. For example, Hatemi et al. (2013) found a relationship between social phobia and political attitudes toward out-groups. Furthermore, genetic analysis showed that such effects occurred not as a result of social conditioning, as might have been expected and predicted by previous political science models, but rather resulting from basic individual differences in inherent levels of baseline fear.

Applying these tools holds obvious implications for treating the increasing numbers of veterans returning from our many conflicts overseas and for reducing the huge social costs of post–traumatic stress disorder and other conditions resulting from exposure to combat. Other avenues might include informing the public about how fear-based political messages activate parts of their biology to inspire or repress action. Without incorporating clinical methods, discovery and categorization of underlying etiological factors, divergent manifestations, and targeted treatment programs will not be developed. Clinical methods have helped support public policy goals that strive to use knowledge and action to achieve solutions to pressing public problems, such as helping veterans struggling to readjust to civilian life.

Other clinical traits of interest, such as the nature of anxiety, aggression, affiliation, and bonding, hold critical import for the ways in which people form political preferences, take part in local community and national elections, and engage in all those behaviors involving citizenship and participation, including war, that are of critical interest to political psychologists. These forces affect how people condition those around them, such as their children, to respond to the political world they confront. While such topics are explored in the political psychology literature, research continues to be conducted largely without the benefit of clinical approaches or measures. Indeed, there are few modern explorations of political traits using a clinical approach in the study of political behavior (for an exception, see Post 1998), although numerous explorations outside that arena of interest exist, pointing to the efficacy and utility of the method. For example, scholars have examined differences in happiness by ideological disposition (Choma, Busseri, and Sadava 2009; Napier and Jost 2008), psychopathology and political aggression (Post 1998), and terrorism and mental pathologies (Tood, Wilson, and Casey 2005; Atran 2003). Whether clinical approaches find a significant relationship or not, the results are critically informative. In the case of terrorism, despite public sentiment that suicide terrorists are "crazed cowards bent on senseless destruction" (Atran 2003, 1534), clinical approaches suggest that terrorists are not dysfunctional or pathological, but rather that "terrorism is basically another form of politically motivated violence that is perpetrated by rational, lucid people who have valid motives" (Ruby 2002, 15). Such knowledge has obvious implications regarding public support for various kinds of antiterror policies.

We have provided only a few examples of how clinical approaches might inform the study of politics. The application of clinical research easily extends into other political domains as well, including such common concerns as the study of leadership, cooperation and aggression, and political participation. In this way, invoking established and validated clinical methods to address a current real problem would allow the study of political behavior to return to one of its original intentions of demonstrating applied policy relevance.

Developmental Psychology

Despite early forays into the area investigating the psychological processes by which children become politically socialized (Greenstein and Tarrow 1970; Niemi and Jennings 1991), developmental approaches represent perhaps the most underappreciated subfield of political psychology. This may be due in part to the multifaceted and complex nature by which individuals develop from infancy to adulthood, encompassing prenatal care, infancy, childhood, puberty, and adolescence, or may be from the misperception that these questions were "asked and answered" developmental processes involving nutrition, socialization, parenting, and neurobiology, at the least. The seminal contributions by M. Kent Jennings and colleagues (Langton and Jennings 1968) assumed that parental child concordance resulted from socialization and implied that children did not possess or form their own unique attitudes. However, two psychologists (Hess and Torney 1967) established that children do possess independent attitudes. Their study, *The Development of Political Attitudes in Children*, was based on a novel study of over twelve thousand children from eight major American cities. The findings are critically important for models of political socialization although these studies have remained relatively unaddressed in political psychology (for exceptions, see Torney-Purta and Amadeo 2003; Torney-Purta 2004). A recent article by Hatemi et al. (2009) presented perhaps the most challenging response to early models that privileged processes of socialization in the etiology of political preferences and behavior. In this study, they used a longitudinal sample of children assessed for political attitudes every two years from ages eight to eighteen. Over the course of their childhood, children's attitudes became more coherent, and as they grew older, children answered more of the questions and expressed more opinions on the questions answered. By fifteen, children closely matched the attitude structure, but not necessarily the attitudes, of their mothers. At first, it appeared that children's attitudes were largely socialized during childhood, but the study also found that once children leave home, social forces give way to personal dispositions; genetic similarity, not social upbringing, accounted for parent–child concordance. The findings hold profound implications for understanding parent–child transmission of political attitudes, political cognition and sophistication, and political learning.

While some work on child development has explored the origins of psychopathology (Erikson 1968) and the nature of political socialization in childhood (Greenstein and Tarrow 1970), much less research has focused on the way in which prenatal development affects politically significant behaviors, such as cooperation or aggression. Yet this area of psychology has proven crucial to explicating how the human mind develops throughout our lives, from infancy through childhood and adolescence into adulthood, and holds the key to achieving a better understanding of many aspects of change and constancy in attitudes and behavior over the lifespan.

One example suffices to illustrate the critical importance that development across stages of growth can exert on later behavior. First, prenatal nutrition exerts a significant impact on subsequent child development that can manifest an impact throughout life. Like puberty and menopause, pregnancy itself constitutes an important developmental stage for those experiencing its effects. Children born to mothers who suffer from maternal malnutrition or other severe stresses, such as those that might result from poverty, war, famine, or violence, become much more sensitive to the effects of stress in later life, making them more vulnerable to disease, aggression, and other social ills (Essex et al. 2002). Mothers who suffer from depression during pregnancy risk low birth weight and preterm birth in their offspring (Grote et al. 2010). Anyone who has seen a child with fetal alcohol syndrome or a "crack baby" is aware of the increased risk of numerous physical illnesses resulting from low birth weight, as well as the cognitive, social, learning, and emotional delays, deficits, and impairments that plague these children for life (Elliott et al. 2007). All these limitations serve to isolate affected individuals from peers and adults, leading to enhanced risk for attachment disorders and other personality deficits in addition to whatever cognitive and physiological problems plague them. The quality of prenatal nutrition affects many women in poor and rural parts of the world who are subjected to famine and other forms of physical and social stress during pregnancy. Little is known about the later influence of such forces on the political and social abilities of their children and the way such factors might affect the development of subsequent political institutions in those societies. Yet, given what is known about the negative sequelae of drugs and alcohol on prenatal development, such malnutrition and psychosocial stress likely exerts a similarly powerful effect on subsequent child growth and learning ability, including moral and social learning. These implications have obvious political ramifications, especially because entire populations may be affected. Studies exploring the effect of famine or genocide on the culture, physical growth, psychological development, and attitudes of those subjected to its effects might prove extremely illuminating and provide ammunition to those seeking to ameliorate these effects. For example, the number of infants abandoned or sent to orphanages in eastern Europe reached critical levels in the 1980s due to the severe economic crisis. In certain orphanages, infants were left alone for twenty-three hours a day without affection or stimulation. As a result, they developed significant deficits in a wide variety of domains, including language and the ability to experience normal human empathy and attachment. Such deficits not only encompassed learning deficiencies, but also resulted in stunted neurological development. Simply put their brains did not develop as they should have. Effects included deficient glucose metabolism and impaired neural function (Chugani et al. 2001; Eluvathingal et al. 2006). These conditions lead to impaired function of the neural network that affects emotional, learning, affective, empathic, and other cognitive functions. As far as we know, not a single study in political behavior has explored prenatal conditions as predictors for later life political behavior, despite the critical importance of biological, psychological, and physiological development for all aspects of human behavior.

Including developmental approaches can help us to understand how nutrition and other aspects of prenatal care can affect the propensity for violence and resilience in populations subjected to starvation, famine, or other systematic forms of stress such as forced migration. No one has yet applied the findings above to large-scale social ills such as famine and war, or examined how such effects might lead to permanent changes in brain structure and function in offspring due to malnutrition, lack of social attention, or chronic stress and fear. These forces can be even more severe and endemic in certain regions or populations. For example, rather than tens of thousands of infants being abandoned in eastern Europe for several years, the refugee situation in the Sudan represents a case where hundreds of thousands of infants and children are denied both nutrition and attention over decades. The long-term political ramifications remain unknown.

Here we show that instantiations of historically useful models and methods drawn from developmental and clinical psychology can continue to inform our future understanding of the foundations and manifestations of political behavior, just as they have in the past. In particular, we suggest that developmental approaches can further our appreciation for the various ways in which environmental factors such as poverty and violence can affect the neurobiological and social development of children, which can exert profound influences on adult political behavior. In addition, clinical approaches can deepen the contextualization of our knowledge of critical dynamics involving the influence of personality on politics, anxiety, and fear. Such a perspective can also explicate individual variance in the expression of other emotions that can in turn affect susceptibility to various forms of political messaging, including campaign advertising, and the subtle interplay between leadership, followership, dominance, aggression, and cooperation. Both approaches provide not only a means to understand behavior, but also a way to explicate potential mechanisms to engage and specially address problems of human suffering.

References

Adorno, T. W., Else Frenkel-Brunswik, Daniel J. Levinson, and R. Nevitt Sanford. 1950. *The Authoritarian Personality*. New York: Harper and Row.

Ainsworth, Mary S., and John Bowlby. 1991. "An Ethological Approach to Personality Development." *American Psychologist* 46:333–41.

Altemeyer, Robert. 1981. *Right-Wing Authoritarianism*. Winnipeg: University of Manitoba Press.

Antony, Martin M., Karen Rowa, Andrea Liss, Stephen R. Swallow, and Richard P. Swinson. 2005. "Social Comparison Processes in Social Phobia." *Behavior Therapy* 36:65–75.

Arendt, Hannah. 1963. *Eichmann in Jerusalem: A Report on the Banality of Evil*. New York: Viking.

Asch, Solomon E. 1955. "Opinions and Social Pressure." *Scientific American* 193 (5): 31–35.

Atran, Scott. 2003. "Genesis of Suicide Terrorism." *Science* 299:1534–39.

Balter, Michael. 2010. "When Social Fear Disappears, So Does Racism." *Science Now*, April 12, http://www.sciencemag.org/news/2010/04/when-social-fear-disappears-so-does-racism.

Bizer, George Y., Jon A. Krosnick, Allyson L. Holbrook, S. Christian Wheeler, Derek D. Rucker, and Richard E. Petty. 2004. "The Impact of Personality on Cognitive, Behavioral, and Affective Political Processes: The Effects of Need to Evaluate." *Journal of Personality* 72 (5): 995–1028.

Bouchard, Thomas J., David T. Lykken, Matthew McGue, Nancy L. Segal, and Auke Tellegen. 1990. "Sources of Human Psychological Differences: The Minnesota Study of Twins Reared Apart." *Science* 250:223–28.

Bouchard, Thomas J., and Matt McGue. 2003. "Genetic and Environmental Influences on Human Psychological Differences." *Journal of Neurobiology* 54:4–45.

Brader, Ted. 2005. "Striking a Responsive Chord: How Political Ads Motivate and Persuade Voters by Appealing to Emotions." *American Journal of Political Science* 49:388–405.

Brown, Roger. 1986. *Social Psychology*. 2nd ed. New York: Free Press.

Campbell, Angus, Philip E. Converse, Warren E. Miller, and Donald E. Stokes. 1960. *The American Voter*. New York: Wiley.

Caprara, Gian Vittorio, Shalom Schwartz, Cristina Capanna, Michele Vecchione, and Claudio Barbaranelli. 2006. "Personality and Politics: Values, Traits, and Political Choice." *Political Psychology* 27 (1): 1–28.

Carney, Dana R., John T. Jost, Samuel D. Gosling, and Jeff Potter. 2008. "The Secret Lives of Liberals and Conservatives: Personality Profiles, Interaction Styles, and the Things They Leave Behind." *Political Psychology* 29 (6): 807–40.

Choma, Becky L., Michael A. Busseri, and Stanley W. Sadava. 2009. "Liberal and Conservative Political Ideologies: Different Routes to Happiness?" *Journal of Research in Personality* 43 (3): 502–5.

Chugani, Harry T., Michael E. Behen, Otto Muzik, Csaba Juhász, Ferenc Nagy, and Diane C. Chugani. 2001. "Local Brain Funcational Activity Following Early

Deprivation: A Study of Postinstitutionalized Romanian Orphans." *Neuroimage* 14:1290–1301.

Costa, Paul, and Robert R. McCrae. 1985. *The NEO Personality Inventory: Manual Form S and Form R*. Odessa, FL: Psychological Assessment Resources.

Eaves, Lindon J., and Hans J. Eysenck. 1974. "Genetics and the Development of Social Attitudes." *Nature* 249:288–89.

Elliott, E. J., J. Payne, A. Morris, E. Haan, and C. Bower. 2007. "Fetal Alcohol Syndrome: A Prospective National Surveillance Study." *Archives of Disease in Childhood* 93 (9): 732–37.

Eluvathingal, Thomas J., Harry T. Chugani, Michael E. Behen, Csaba Juhász, Otto Muzik, Mohsin Maqbool, Diane C. Chugani, and Malek Makki. 2006. "Abnormal Brain Connectivity in Children after Early Severe Socioemotional Deprivation: A Diffusion Tensor Imaging Study." *Pediatrics* 117:2093–2100.

Erikson, Erik H. 1968. *Identity: Youth and Crisis*. New York: W. W. Norton.

Essex, Marilyn J., Marjorie H. Klein, Eunsuk Cho, and Ned H. Kalin. 2002. "Maternal Stress Beginning in Infancy May Sensitize Children to Later Stress Exposure: Effects on Cortisol and Behavior." *Biological Psychiatry* 52 (8): 776–84.

Eysenck, Hans J. 1947. *Dimensions of Personality*. London: Kegan Paul, Trench, Trubner.

——. 1954. *The Psychology of Politics*. London: Routledge.

——. 1990. "Biological Dimensions of Personality." In *Handbook of Personality: Theory and Research*, edited by Lawrence A. Pervin, 249–76. New York: Guilford.

Eysenck, Hans J., and Glenn D. Wilson. 1978. *The Psychological Basis of Ideology*. Baltimore: University Park Press.

George, Alexander L., and Juliette L. George. 1956. *Woodrow Wilson and Colonel House: A Personality Study*. New York: John Day.

Gerber, Alan S., Gregory A. Huber, David Doherty, Conor M. Dowling, and Shang E. Ha. 2010. "Personality and Political Attitudes: Relationships across Issue Domains and Political Contexts." *American Political Science Review* 104:111–33.

Greenstein, Fred I., and Sidney Tarrow. 1970. *Political Orientations of Children: The Use of Semi-Projective Technique in Three Nations*. Beverly Hills: Sage.

Grote, Nancy K., Jeffrey A. Bridge, Amelia R. Gavin, Jennifer L. Melville, Satish Iyengar, and Wayne J. Katon. 2010. "A Meta-analysis of Depression during Pregnancy and the Risk of Preterm Birth, Low Birth Weight, and Intrauterine Growth Restriction." *Archives of General Psychiatry* 67 (10): 1012–24.

Hatemi, Peter K., Carolyn L. Funk, Sarah E. Medland, Hermine M. Maes, Judy L. Silberg, Nicholas G. Martin, and Lindon J. Eaves. 2009. "Genetic and Environmental Transmission of Political Attitudes over a Life Time." *Journal of Politics* 71 (3): 1141–56.

Hatemi, Peter K., Rose McDermott, Lindon J. Eaves, Kenneth S. Kendler, and Michael C. Neale. 2013. "Fear as a Disposition and an Emotional State: A Genetic and Environmental Approach to Out-Group Political Preferences." *American Journal of Political Science* 57:279–93.

Hess, Robert D., and Judith V. Torney. 1967. *The Development of Political Attitudes in Children*. Chicago: Aldine.

Jost, John T., Jack Glaser, Arie W. Kruglanski, and Frank J. Sulloway. 2003. "Political Conservatism as Motivated Social Cognition." *Psychological Bulletin* 129 (3): 339–75.

Jost, John T., Jaime L. Napier, Hulda Thorisdottir, Samuel D. Gosling, Tibor Palfai, and Brian Ostafin. 2007. "Are Needs to Manage Uncertainty and Threat Associated with Political Conservatism or Ideological Extremity?" *Personality and Social Psychology Bulletin* 33:989–1007.

Kendler, Kenneth S., Michael C. Neale, Ronald C. Kessler, Andrew C. Heath, and Lindon J. Eaves. 1992. "The Genetic Epidemiology of Phobias in Women: The Interrelationship of Agoraphobia, Social Phobia, Situational Phobia, and Simple Phobia." *Archives of General Psychiatry* 49 (4): 273–81.

Langton, Kenneth P., and M. Kent Jennings. 1968. "Political Socialization and the High School Curriculum in the United States." *American Political Science Review* 62:852–67.

Lasswell, Harold D. 1930. *Psychopathology and Politics*. Chicago: University of Chicago Press.

Lazarsfeld, Paul F., Bernard Berelson, and Hazel Gaudet. 1968. *The People's Choice: How the Voter Makes up His Mind in a Presidential Campaign*. New York: Columbia University Press.

Lipset, Seymour Martin, Paul F. Lazarsfeld, A. H. Barton, and J. Linz. 1954. "The Psychology of Voting: An Analysis of Political Behavior." In *Handbook of Social Psychology*, edited by Gardner Lindzey, 2:1124–75. Reading, MA: Addison-Wesley.

McClosky, Herbert, Jr., and Charles A. Bann. 1979. "On the Reappraisal of the Classical Conservatism Scale." *Political Methodology* 6:149–72.

Milgram, Stanley. 1974. *Obedience to Authority: An Experimental View*. New York: HarperCollins.

Mondak, Jeffrey J., Matthew V. Hibbing, Damarys Canache, Mitchell A. Seligson, and Mary R. Anderson. 2010. "Personality and Civic Engagement: An Integrative Framework for the Study of Trait Effects on Political Behavior." *American Political Science Review* 104:85–110.

Moscovici, Serge, Gabriel Mugny, and Eddy van Avermaet, eds. 1985. *Perspectives on Minority Influence*. Cambridge: Cambridge University Press.

Napier, Jaime L., and John T. Jost. 2008. "Why Are Conservatives Happier than Liberals?" *Psychological Science* 19:565–72.

National Institutes of Health. 2011. "Interdisciplinary Research." http://commonfund.nih.gov/interdisciplinary/overview.aspx.

Nemeth, Charlan J. 1986. "Differential Contributions of Majority and Minority Influence." *Psychological Review* 93:23–32.

Niemi, Richard G., and M. Kent Jennings. 1991. "Issues and Inheritance in the Formation of Party Identification." *American Journal of Political Science* 35:970–88.

Phelps, Elizabeth A., and Laura A. Thomas. 2003. "Race, Behavior, and the Brain: The Role of Neuroimaging in Understanding Complex Social Behaviors." *Political Psychology* 24 (4): 747–58.

Post, Jerrold M. 1998. "Terrorist Psycho-Logic: Terrorist Behavior as a Consequence of Psychological Forces." In *Origins of Terrorism: Psychologies, Ideologies, Theologies,*

States of Mind, edited by Walter Reich, 25–40. Washington, DC: Woodrow Wilson Center Press.

Ruby, Charles L. 2002. "Are Terrorists Mentally Deranged?" *Analyses of Social Issues and Public Policy* 2:15–26.

Schiller, Daniela, Marie-H. Monfils, Candace M. Raio, David C. Johnson, Joseph E. LeDoux, and Elizabeth A. Phelps. 2010. "Preventing the Return of Fear in Humans Using Reconsolidation Update Mechanisms." *Nature* 463:49–53.

Tood, Anna, J. Clare Wilson, and Sharon N. Casey. 2005. "Comparing British and Australian Fear of Terrorism Pre and Post the Iraqi War." *Psychiatry, Psychology and the Law* 12 (1): 184–93.

Torney-Purta, Judith. 2004. "Adolescents' Political Socialization in Changing Contexts: An International Study in the Spirit of Nevitt Sanford." *Political Psychology* 25 (3): 465–78.

Torney-Purta, Judith, and Jo-Ann Amadeo. 2003. "A Cross-National Analysis of Political and Civic Involvement among Adolescents." *PS: Political Science and Politics* 36:269–74.

Van Hiel, Alain, Mario Pandelaere, and Bart Duriez. 2004. "The Impact of Need for Closure on Conservative Beliefs and Racism: Differential Mediation by Authoritarian Submission and Authoritarian Dominance." *Personality and Social Psychology Bulletin* 30:824–37.

Verhulst, Brad, Peter K. Hatemi, and Nicholas G. Martin. 2010. "The Nature of the Relationship between Personality Traits and Political Attitudes." *Personality and Individual Differences* 49:306–16.

Wilson, Glenn D. 1973. *The Psychology of Conservatism*. London: Academic Press.

Wilson, Glenn D, and John R. Patterson. 1968. "A New Measure of Conservatism." *British Journal of Clinical Psychology* 7:264–69.

Zimbardo, Philip G. 2007. *The Lucifer Effect: Understanding How Good People Turn Evil*. New York: Random House.

3

Polygyny and Violence against Women

Rose McDermott and Jonathan Cowden

Many discussions about the origins of terrorism highlight divides between the liberal, democratic, industrialized West and other parts of the world. Indeed, whether derived from politics, economics, religion, or history, some degree of resentment toward the West and Western values is no doubt fueled by struggles over land, resources, power, and preferred institutions for political and economic structures (e.g., Lewis 1993; Huntington 1997; Rashid 2000; Kepel 2002). If these were the only sources of enmity, the search for peace would be difficult enough. But the problem is worsened by a potent and often unappreciated element of cultural friction: the fundamental clash of values surrounding the appropriate role of women in society. This clash emerges entirely independently of economic and political contests, although those issues often serve to fuel such conflicts and should be confronted directly, without shaping our analysis to suit political correctness. This we do in this chapter. Because Western values often encourage a foundation of at least legal equality between the sexes, threats to the assumed sociopolitical dominance of men in areas that strongly espouse these traditions provoke systematic hostility and opposition. As a result, we suggest that the original construction of the source of division is the wrong one to pose. Rather than counterposing East against West, arguing about the clash of civilizations in the prototypical Huntington sense (1997), the critical concern should actually revolve around the sources and consequences of violence by men toward women as the root of conflict both within and between nations. What are some of the origins of the violence that men direct toward women? Is it simply rooted in male sexual desire for women and the anger and frustration that may result when men hold women responsible for men's own drives? Or do men seek to control women simply because they are physically and financially stronger and they are able to get away with exerting power over those with fewer resources? Alternatively, does male violence emerge from a much broader array of social incentives and permissions? And what are the consequences of such violence, not only for women and children, but also for the men who instigate it and for the societies that sanction it? These patterns of violence often begin in the home and serve as models for the assumed hierarchical relationships between the sexes, as well as implicit endorsement for dominance, coercion, and violence as the proper form of conflict resolution in society more broadly.

We argue here that female financial and social independence are feared not merely because of their material effects, but also because of the threat they pose to the cultural values, status, and personal power of many men, particularly in underdeveloped and developing regions of the world. Specifically, the emancipation of women erodes men's control over their own families, in ways that are potentially culturally humiliating and emotionally painful for men, especially those emanating from a tradition of strong patriarchy. In short, the prospect of liberated women threatens male status. Further, liberalism often also threatens the position of senior women in these developing societies, women who are allowed to dominate junior women, such as daughters and daughters-in-law, as well as junior men, including sons. Note here that men are not necessarily the primary guardians of a culture that oppresses women in these circumstances; women actively participate in such repression because they refuse to give up control over those few cultural areas, such as control inside the home, to which they have been assigned by men, including circumscribing the activities of their female family members. The prospect of female emancipation therefore provides a potent source of male—and sometimes even female—opposition to more secular or democratic movements, particularly in more patriarchal societies.

This process is exacerbated by the common practice of patrilocality, whereby women move to the town, village, or home of their husbands, often leaving behind the fathers, brothers, or uncles who might protect them if they lived closer to home. Without such protection from family members, the only prospect many women have for protection from abusive relatives is to give birth to sons, who are valued by the father's family. These sons, in turn, may prove loyal to these mothers. But such a family structure further erodes the bonds between husband and wife, since the husband's primary female loyalty often remains with his mother rather than with his wife or his daughters. Such a privileging of parent–child bonds over the marital bond diminishes the possibility for creating models of equality between the sexes for children of such unions.

We define patriarchal societies as those in which men have power over women. Aspects of patriarchal cultures may be explained or exacerbated, at least in part, by patrilocality and polygynist family structures where a man has more than one wife, but are not defined by such characteristics. Recognition of the way in which patrilocality and polygyny each independently and in combination precipitate violence toward women and children in these societies draws attention to the structural problems associated with societies that combine these features and opens some possibilities for ameliorating its effects.

Here we specifically address simultaneous, as opposed to sequential, polygyny because it reduces the availability of young women for young men, posing tremendous consequences for young men's prospects for marriage and reproduction, as well as increasing the risk for political violence (Hudson and den Boer 2002, 2004). We show how this causes increased levels of many forms of violence in and across these areas.

An essential point is that men's desire for patriarchal control of women is not so arbitrary that it can be blown away by a good breath of Western logic, education, or liberalism. Rather, it finds its roots in strong traditions and structures, often endorsed, wrongly or otherwise, by religious beliefs that privilege male power and dominance in all aspects of life. The violent effects emerge from the widespread lifestyle of patriarchy, polygyny, and patrilocality, and therefore have continuing significance in many countries today where such practices continue to dominate cultural and economic traditions. We trace these origins of male power and note their consequences for the lives and status of women throughout the developing world. We do so by discussing the independent effects of patriarchy and polygyny. We then provide a detailed analysis of the impact of these forces on a wide variety of manifestations of violence toward women and children using data derived from the WomanStats Project (www.womanstats.org). At the end we consider the challenges faced by policymakers and human rights advocates who wish to begin to redress such gender inequalities.

Polygyny

To begin, a few definitions are in order. Polygamy includes both polygyny, where one man has many wives, as well as polyandry, where one woman has many husbands. Political issues surrounding laws about polygyny are exacerbated by the cultural and religious circumstances that are often associated with it. Polygyny remains a common practice around the world, existing in more than 83 percent of 849 cultures worldwide; in about 35 percent of cases, such practices are commonly sororal, meaning men marry sisters. Such a practice may be undertaken to help reduce the risk of intermarital tension and hostility among wives or toward children of such unions. Everywhere, the practice is more widespread among high-status, high-wealth men. By contrast, polyandry is found in only four of 849 cultures worldwide, mostly in Nepal, and always co-occurs with polygyny, such that high-status men in such cultures also take multiple wives. In such cultures, polyandry tends to occur only briefly and among low-status men, although it is often fraternal in nature as well.

However, to be clear, the consequences of violence we document here do not extend to polyandry. As a result, we examine polygynous practices where one man has more than one wife simultaneously. Polygyny holds important implications for reproductive success and control, and having children with more than one wife at a time affects this process in ways that differ significantly from having children sequentially with different mates over time. In our analysis, the critical concern revolves around the sources and consequences of violence of men toward women and children and how this affects the tendency toward violence and suppression of civil rights and political liberties within states. This latter phenomenon results in large part from the surplus of men that occurs in polygynous systems where many junior men need to be evicted from the society in order for senior men to have access to multiple wives.

In addition, we are not concerned with simultaneous sexual relationships that do not involve childbearing or prospects for the intergenerational transfer of wealth as a result of the shared economic circumstances that remain intrinsic to legal marriages. That is because there can be two potential uses of the concept of polygyny: the first a social bonding system, and the second a breeding one. It is possible to conceptualize these two types of systems in a two-by-two table. Most mammals, including gorillas for example, have both polygynous social and polygynous breeding systems, whereas there are no species who exhibit a polygynous social system in concert with a monogamous mating structure. By contrast, most birds have monogamous social bonding in the context of polygynous breeding, while a few, including the black vulture, as well as some humans, demonstrate both monogamous bonding and breeding preferences. However, in human systems, such monogamous breeding structures are often socially imposed, as occurs in large complex societies, or ecologically imposed by limited resources that make it prohibitive for men to provide sufficiently for multiple wives or children.

We argue that violence toward women and children and suppression of basic rights can be potentiated by a number of factors, including such things as patriarchy, patrilocality, and polygyny. These cultural features and social structures often go hand in hand and, in combination, enhance male control over women and children in ways that allow, and often encourage, violence and suppression of political rights and liberties. In particular, we demonstrate using detailed empirical data that polygyny is strongly correlated with a wide array of different kinds of violence against women and children, as well as suppression of political rights and liberties, and increased spending on weapons.

Many Westerners argue that it is inappropriate to make value judgments about other cultures' preferences regarding social structures. We analyze the issue of polygyny in terms of basic human rights, and we demonstrate here that such rights in woman and children are fiercely abrogated in societies and cultures where polygyny is present.

The Persistence of Patriarchal Values

In our construction, patriarchal values are promoted by two important features: patrilocality and polygyny. The effects of these variables may appear partly regional, and partly religious, but we postulate that each feature will exert an independent effect on the outcome of interest: violence by men against women and children. For our purposes, we examine this outcome along three separate dimensions: violence against women, violence against children, and state level effects. For the final dimension, we extend our analysis to examine the effect of such marital structures, and the economic, political, and social practices that often accompany them, on civil rights, political freedoms, and weapons procurement, as a proxy for the propensity of the state to consider and model violence as a viable means of conflict resolution between states.

Patriarchy can exert its effects through many subtle and overlapping mechanisms. One of the ways in which this power can manifest is through male control over female marriage. For example, male expectation of control over a daughter's marriage is critical in many societies because a man's economic and social status is importantly determined by his kinswomen's alliances. A man who marries into a family with many strong and wealthy men enhances his ability to protect his flocks and to increase his local status through such an association. Arranged marriages are therefore traditionally preferred to love matches. In the service of maximizing the benefits from a marriage, a woman's value is enhanced by various practices that restrict her own romantic choices and promote her chastity, including claustration (shutting up in a cloister), genital mutilation, and veiling (Weisfeld 1993). Control is supported by stringent punishments for women who flout cultural norms.

While the degree to which men exert literal physical control over women in particular societies remains contingent on a whole host of sociological and economic factors, men retain control over the vast majority of physical resources needed to survive, including money and property (Mealey 2000; Rosen 1978). This often becomes instantiated in family law customs and practices that restrict female ability to marry someone of her choosing, divorce an abusive husband, retain custody of children following an imposed divorce, or inherit property. In many parts of the world, men's lives exist primarily in the public sphere while women's lives still remain largely confined to the household. Ironically, this segregation of sexes can lead to a remarkable degree of female independence over their own social lives and worlds within the home (Fallers and Fallers 1976). Nevertheless, women continue to be restricted in their public movements from the time of puberty in many developing countries. Such limitation prevents many women from being able to get an education or to achieve financial independence through employment. Instead, women often remain at the mercy of those men who can provide for their sustenance.

A woman's position in these societies thus becomes largely determined by her marriage. But because divorce is so common, and can be granted by male fiat in many areas, women's position in the hierarchy remains tenuous at best (Mealey 2000; Rosen 1978); indeed, in many parts of the world, men often retain control of all important resources following divorce, including custody of any children, while women revert to the status of property in the hands of other male relatives. Whatever security a woman has results from the formal nature of her marriage contract and the strength of her family of origin, particularly her male relatives, in the particular area, which is why patrilocality imposes such insecurity on so many women. Any man can be dishonored by threats to the chastity and virtue of his female relatives, and killings of honor on behalf of these women may be committed by brothers, fathers, or husbands in order to retain family status. However, fathers most often blame their daughters, and not the perpetrator, for violations of purity (Fallers and Fallers 1976).

A man uses his control to ensure that a woman marries not just to her advantage (as he perceives it), but more important to the advantage of himself and his male kin. A woman marrying below her social status dishonors her family, whereas her marriage into a large and high-status kin group creates or cements a relationship of social importance for her entire family. He, or other male relatives, might benefit in other ways as well. For example, by exchanging his daughter for a wife for himself or a male relative, a man might use his control over a daughter to get an extra bride, and thus increase his own reproductive advantage by making it possible to have more sons. Equally, he could resolve a blood feud by giving a woman in marriage. Or, by obtaining as high a bride-price as possible, he increases his wealth and thus his own future marriage prospects.

Thus, male control over women under his dominion constitutes a key part of his family life as well as his social and economic status. Since his women increase in value with their modesty and chastity, it is vital for him to control their behavior around other men. Women also participate in enforcing and perpetuating these standards by often "out-bidding" each other in seeking to appear pious in order to improve their marriage prospects. This phenomenon clearly contributes to the high divorce rate in many of these areas as men come to find out that, once married, their wives may try to break out of the strict standards they adhered to prior to marriage. Yet a woman who did not adhere to such standards prior to marriage would reduce her prospects, since her male relatives would not be able to secure her a higher-status marriage partner. By contrast, there has traditionally been "no objection to a man marrying a woman of lower status, since the woman, in the view of the jurists, is in any case inferior, and no social damage could therefore result from such a marriage" (Lewis 1995, 180). This partly results from the inherent value placed on female beauty, which exists independent of social status, and also from the fact that the real value a woman offers to a man lies in the number and physical strength of her male kinfolk and offspring, which is another reason why infertile women in such societies often become particularly vulnerable.

It is therefore inevitable that when confronted with attempts to promote women's political, economic, or sexual independence, men from traditional cultures, espousing conservative expectations about patriarchal control, will feel threatened and resentful. And, as noted above, men are not the only ones whose positions may be threatened. Senior women, who retain control over their daughters-in-law and young sons, may also find their positions compromised by any threat to the existing patriarchal system.

However, as Kandiyoti argues, inherent contradictions lie at the root of certain types of patriarchy, and in the end, polygyny and the subjugation of women "ultimately mutilate and distort the male psyche" (1994, 198). This results from the complex dynamic between the sexes in societies where the marital bond remains weak relative to the mother–child bond or bonds within sexes. Societies where men feel a stronger loyalty to their mothers than their wives encourage violence toward junior women by senior women who know that their sons will not oppose their actions. In addition, polygyny means that there will not be enough women to provide mates for lower-status men, who will likely remain childless.

Those who work for female equality commonly assume that education or modernism will erode such attitudes and values, but history shows the resilience of entrenched cultural traditions that validate, instantiate, and perpetuate patriarchal control. Although the French Revolution inspired widespread debate about the emancipation of women, it led to little change for women compared to men. For example, even in the wake of the French Revolution's ostensible commitment to liberty and equality, there has been persistent resistance to change in women's attire. Even in Turkey, Atatürk never prohibited the veil, though he banned the fez; and Islamic revival has been notably associated with a return by women, but not men, to traditional dress in Turkey and elsewhere (Lewis 1995). Likewise, there is no evidence that such consequences of modernization as the acquisition of wealth or exposure to Western ideas reduce the patriarchal value system. Thus "the emancipation of women is one of the main grievances of the fundamentalists and its reversal is in the forefront of their programme" (Lewis 1995, 382). A fundamental clash of values over the rights of women relative to men will therefore not be resolved by anything as straightforward as economic globalization or improvements in literacy. A deeper understanding of the nature of resentment toward female independence and equality must incorporate a realistic account of why patriarchal control is so highly valued by so many men, particularly in polygynous societies.

One school sees patriarchy as essentially arbitrary, emerging from specific historical events that no longer justify its maintenance. Women's political marginalization and loss of freedom has been traced, for example, to the eighth and ninth centuries, when international conquests and the acquisition of women slaves gave men exceptional power in sexual politics (Mernissi 1987). This perspective implies that if modern men are presented with enough pressure for equality, they may be persuaded to abandon their old-fashioned ideals. But the strong resistance that many men have shown to women's increasing independence and striving for equality suggests the alternative view that we propose. In our view, patriarchal control is not merely the arbitrary remnant of a temporary historical culture, but it is rather intimately associated with the prevailing family structure, economic system, and access to reproductive rights and freedoms. For example, Tertilt finds that "banning polygyny decreases fertility by 40 percent, increases savings by 70 percent, and increases output per capita by 170 percent" (2005, 1341).

Ironically, it appears to be the case that societies where women possess more productive value, and are thus more independent, including agricultural ones, produce higher rates of polygyny (Lesthaeghe et al. 1994). This seems to be the case because women in these societies must balance their productive and reproductive responsibilities wisely. Long periods of postpartum abstinence (over a year) accomplish this goal, while encouraging male polygyny. In essence, different women take turns with the same man to balance their productive and reproductive activities through polygynous processes.

Giving a kinswoman in marriage is one important mechanism for alliance formation. In particular, male children of such unions establish strong incentives for each side of the family to invest in the resources that will go to those children. In these circumstances, the high value that a man places on his control of women is no whim. Rather, it is central to his ability to function effectively as a father and family provider (Weisfeld 1993). Control over women confers status precisely because it ensures paternity over her children and thus helps establish and cement networks of control.

Polygyny and Male Violence

Wealth-based polygyny is widespread. Polygyny can be potentiated by other sources as well, such as the uneven accumulation of wealth in, for example, oil-based economies. The results are in some cases extreme. The Crown Princes of Saudi Arabia, defined as the male descendants of Ibn Saud (who founded the country and died in 1953), are estimated to number between six thousand and seven thousand. Not only does polygyny increase the number of unmarried men, but the uneven wealth distribution that accompanies it presents a further predictor of violence. For example, the Gini coefficient of inequality across household incomes accounts for most of the difference between homicide rates among the ten Canadian provinces and fifty U.S. states (Daly and Wilson 1999). Polygyny is concentrated everywhere in the wealthier families and leads to an accumulation of unmarried men in poorer classes.

Polygyny therefore has the unfortunate consequence of generating a class of people—young unmarried men—who are statistically inclined to violence. For example, most homicides in Canada and the United States result from the actions of males aged fifteen to thirty-five; among those, the majority are committed by men between the ages of twenty and twenty-nine; and of those, the majority are committed by unmarried men (Daly and Wilson 1999). In his study of the relationship between single men and social violence in American history, David Courtwright argues that "where married men have been scarce or parental supervision wanting, violence and disorder have flourished, as in the mining camps, cattle towns, Chinatowns, black ghettos, and the small hours of the morning. But when stable family life has been the norm for men and boys, violence and disorder have diminished. . . . What we should not doubt is the social utility of the family, the institution best suited to shape, control, and sublimate the energies of young men" (1996, 280). Similarly in India, districts with higher ratios of men to women have higher rates of homicide (Drèze and Khera 2000).

This phenomenon has both a social and a physiological basis. Mazur and Booth (1998) report that men with high levels of testosterone, including unmarried men, are more likely to exhibit violent and antisocial behaviors, including getting into trouble with the law, substance abuse, and other forms of aggressive behavior. This is at least in part because testosterone acts in the face of challenge, especially threats to social status. Unmarried men searching for mates are more likely to get involved in intrasexual competition with other men, which can easily turn violent. In addition, Mazur shows that age-adjusted testosterone is not constant over time. Rather, male testosterone increases in the years surrounding divorce and decreases in the years surrounding marriage, independent of age. But male testosterone drops in the time surrounding courtship and marriage and drops further with the birth of each child (Gray et al. 2002). Thus, men married to women receive beneficent effects on their propensity toward violence and aggression relative to unmarried men. Mazur and Michalek (1998) argue that this phenomenon helps explain both the low criminality found in married men and the high rates of domestic abuse seen in cases of divorce. This greater propensity toward violence in young men is likely supported, at least in part, by the higher baseline levels of testosterone found within these age ranges.

The presence of large numbers of young unmarried men can arise not only from polygyny but also from distorted overall sex ratios, deriving from such factors as sex-selected abortion, female infanticide, high rates of maternal death in childbirth, and poorer health treatment for women. High sex ratios of men to women occur, for example, in regions such as Afghanistan and Pakistan, as well as other countries such as India and China. High sex ratios have historically been associated with intrasociety violence, aggressive foreign policy initiatives, and governments that, being aware of the threat to the stability of their own regime posed by organizations of unmarried men, tended to be repressive and authoritarian (Hudson and den Boer 2002). But here we concentrate on the independent effect of polygyny on violence specifically directed toward women and children, as well the independent effect of polygyny on the state. Polygyny remains problematic in this regard because for every man who has more than one wife, another man may not be able to find any wife at all.

Even terrorist groups understand the threat posed by large numbers of unmarried men. One of the most notorious terrorist groups ever, the Black September movement, conducted the seizure of Israeli athletes at the Munich Olympics in 1972. When Yassar Arafat's organization sought to dismantle this group for fear that their violence would undermine broader political objectives, military leaders decided to simply marry them off. Through a system of financial incentives and structured "mixers," members of Black September married attractive young Palestinian women. When such men were later asked to leave the country with legal passports, not a single one agreed to go, for fear of losing his family because of past terrorist activities (Hoffman 2001). The Northern Ireland Prison Service used similar strategies when they offered early release to former Irish Republican Army and loyalist terrorists. None of the men offered early parole through a system designed to reaffirm family ties ever returned to prison (Hoffman 2001). The larger point remains that unmarried men simply have less to lose. They also have more incentive to seek dominance through less conventional and more dangerous means, in hopes of garnering the resources required to attract sexual partners.

Entirely aside from international power struggles, therefore, polygynous societies contain the basis for violent response toward women and children. The combination of distorted sex ratios, particularly in the poorer classes, and relatively large wealth differentials means that resentment and anger toward women can be predictably fueled with a ready supply of frustrated, risk-prone young men. When this mixture is added to a volatile political system, the dangers become obvious.

Analysis of WomanStats Data

Here we use a unique data source, the WomanStats Project, to provide a substantial cross-cultural analysis of (1) the impact of polygynous relationships on women's equality; (2) the impact of polygynous relationships on children, including child brides and the children of polygamous unions; and (3) the impact of polygynous relationships on the nation-state.

Polygynous mating systems are known to promote intensified male/ male competition for females and tend to restrict options for females because of male coercion. We examine the link between polygyny and the physical security of women and children using a unique dataset of 171 countries. Controlling for the independent effects of gross domestic product (GDP) and sex ratio, we find statistically significant relationships between polygyny and the following: discrepancy between law and practice concerning women's equality; birth rate; rates of primary and secondary education for male and female children; difference between males and females in HIV infection; age of marriage; maternal mortality; life expectancy; sex trafficking; female genital mutilation; domestic violence; inequity in the treatment of males and females before the law; defense expenditures; and political rights and civil liberties. Elevated frequency of polygynous marriage thus tends to be associated with increases in behavioral constraints and physical costs experienced by women and children in particular. Since our results control for relative wealth (GDP), these costs appear to be due, at least in part, to structural and institutional attempts to control female sexuality and reproduction independent of economic constraints.

Data and Methods

The WomanStats Project (www.womanstats.org) provides national data on polygyny and most of the effects we examine here. Data used in this paper are sampled from 171 countries for the period 2000 to 2007. We used year-matched data when available. Our maximum gap between data samples was five years, a short period compared to rates of societal change. The WomanStats database provides the largest compilation of information on the status of women in the world, coding over

260 variables for 174 countries. Because we limited our observations to countries with populations over two hundred thousand, we restricted our analysis to 171 of these countries. The preponderance of data came from scholarly research, nongovernmental organization and intergovernmental organization reports, governmental reports, and national statistical bureaus, with each piece of information being fully indexed as to source. The WomanStats Project constitutes a unique data set that provides extensive information about women's issues around the world. No other data set on women's issues in the world ranks its equal, whether in terms of the breadth and depth of its coverage, the degree of its reliability checks, or the time spent in its creation. It is literally the best of its kind and permits a comprehensive, comparative statistical analysis unlike any other.

The data on the nation-state come from two well-respected international organizations whose main goal is to collect the information we examine. The data on arms expenditures come from the Stockholm International Peace Research Institute (SIPRI). SIPRI describes themselves as "an independent international institute dedicated to research into conflict, armaments, arms control, and disarmament" although they are supported, in part, by the Swedish government. Their data exist free on the web at www.sipri.org, which is where we obtained these data. They are widely considered to be an unbiased and world-class resource for this material. The information regarding political freedoms and civil liberties comes from Freedom House, an independent nongovernmental organization widely considered to provide the most accurate and comprehensive data on social and political freedoms for countries around the globe. Their information can be accessed at www.freedomhouse.org, which is where we obtained the data.

A total of seventeen outcome variables are considered here, comprising a rich variety of dimensions of women's lives, children's lives, and the influence on the nation-state, aggregated to the level of the state. Taken together, these variables show the profound, systematic, and negative influence of polygyny on women's health and equality, children's welfare, and the nation-state.

Naturally, the state is not the only unit of analysis; ethnic enclaves present another alternative, for instance. But states constitute the basic unit of analysis in the international system and add comparative context to unique or anecdotal case material, particularly so when measures of the variables, such as polygyny, are arguably and reasonably homogeneous across the subunits that a state encompasses.

The variables analyzed below constitute the group of outcomes hypothesized to be most likely affected by polygyny. In other words, given how polygyny affects factors such as sex ratio imbalance as discussed above, and given its inherent incentives and demands, it was possible to generate hypotheses about which factors related to women, children, and the nation-state might be affected by polygyny.

It is not possible to test every variable for its relationship to polygyny, so we test here those that appear most theoretically plausible and empirically tractable. For instance, we can hypothesize that polygyny is likely to lead to higher rates of prostitution, but we cannot test for this relationship because we do not have enough data on rates of prostitution around the world to make it possible to examine this variable statistically. This does not mean that a significant relationship does not exist or might not be uncovered in the future when more comprehensive data on other dependent variables might become available; it just means that we cannot know whether or not a statistically significant relationship exists currently because we are lacking the data to test it. So we must remain agnostic, barring additional data on whether or not such a relationship exists. In addition, there may be other factors affected by polygyny that exist but that we did not know or think to test or report here. However, every relationship discussed below fell within the conventional accepted standard for a statistically significant effect given a prior hypothesis. This means that the likelihood that such relationships occurred by chance and are actually unrelated to polygyny remains very, very low.

In this analysis, it is very important that we control for other variables that might directly cause the outcomes we examine. In particular, we need to control for the effect of GDP, measured in U.S. dollars, on the relationship between polygyny and the other issues we examine. This is because other streams of literature have long indicated a strong relationship between economic development and other aspects of women's rights. If poor outcomes toward women are entirely attributable to poverty, then naturally polygyny does not exert an impact, though such might be erroneously concluded if sole attention were paid to polygyny in the quantitative analysis. But controlling for GDP allows for an independent analysis of the influence of polygyny on the outcome variables concerning equity that comprise our concern. Combined, these two characteristics constitute an incredibly powerful tool for the study of polygyny. We deductively assess the hypothesized relationship between cause (polygyny) and effect (say, domestic violence), and we do so all other things, including the wealth of a country as measured by GDP, being equal.

Results of Analysis

The polygyny variable categorizes countries according to its prevalence. Countries were divided into five categories, ranging from places where polygyny is illegal and uncommon to places where it is legal and common, meaning more than 25 percent of women exist in such unions.

We begin with the variable called discrepancy. Discrepancy is a variable that taps (1) whether a country's laws are in concordance with the United Nations Convention on the Elimination of All Forms of Discrimination against Women (CEDAW) and (2) whether the country enforces these laws. We use the 2007 coding of this variable in this analysis. In the lowest category are those countries where CEDAW-consonant laws exist and are enforced while the highest category refers to countries in which CEDAW-consonant laws are not present or are not enforced. Intrastate conduct that is not consonant with CEDAW does occur more often in more polygynous societies.

Figure 3.1 displays the following: a scatter of the data displaying the actual values of discrepancy and polygyny; the line of best fit, which indicates a strong positive relationship between polygyny and discrepancy, as expected; and the confidence interval portraying the accuracy of prediction.

Further evidence of the effect of polygyny comes in the form of a multiple regression controlling for GDP. The fit statistic used here is distributed $F (2, 129) = 75.62$, and this is of the magnitude that indicates that the variables are not jointly 0, at a high level of significance ($p<0.0005$). There is more evidence of an association, namely, $R^2 = 0.54$.

Polygyny retains an effect in the context of a multiple regression. The multiple regression coefficient for polygyny is positive ($\beta = 0.240888$), and the two-tailed significance test of the null hypothesis can be rejected far beyond the conventional standard ($p<0.0005$). Thus, there is strong confirmation of the role of polygyny. As polygyny goes up, discrepancy rises.

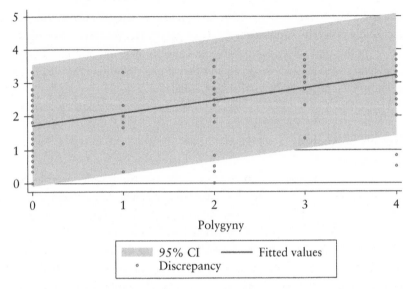

Figure 3.1. Scatterplot, Line of Best Fit, and Confidence Intervals for Discrepancy by Polygyny

Note: A bivariate regression was used to calculate the line of best fit while CI is the uncertainty of prediction.

TABLE 3.1. Effect of Polygyny and GDP on Discrepancy and Births per 1000

Variable	Discrepancy			Births per 1000		
	Coefficient	S.E.	*p*-value	Coefficient	S.E.	*p*-value
Polygyny	0.240888	0.045434	<0.0005	4.690576	0.426328	<0.0005
GDP	−0.000038	0.000005	<0.0005	−0.000234	0.000044	<0.0005
N		132			170	
	F (2, 129) = 75.62, *p*<0.0005			F (2, 167) = 109.23, *p*<0.0005		
R^2		0.54			0.57	

Notes: Coefficients, associated standard errors, *p*-values, and fit statistics from ordinary least squares (ols) regressions with discrepancy and births per 1000 respectively as dependent variables and polygyny and GDP in each of the regressions as independent variables. For discrepancy, the effect of polygyny can be interpreted as follows: each unit increase in polygyny increases discrepancy by 0.24 units, GDP controlled. The coefficient for polygyny in births per 1000 indicates that for each unit increase in polygyny, birth rates go up by 4.69 units, GDP controlled. Interpret other ols coefficients in the same manner.

Women in polygynous countries have more children, on average, than women in less polygynous states. Figure 3.2 presents the same visuals as Figure 3.1, and with the same punch line: polygyny substantially shapes the number of births per one thousand women per year in a state. The fit

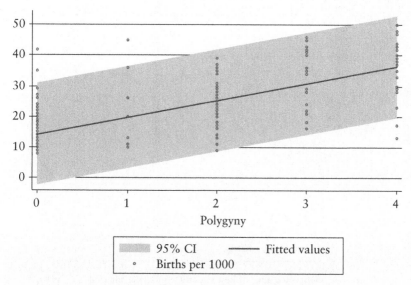

Figure 3.2. Scatterplot, Line of Best Fit, and Confidence Intervals for
Births Per 1000 by Polygyny

Note: A bivariate regression was used to calculate the line of best fit while CI is the
uncertainty of prediction.

statistic with $F\ (2,\ 167) = 109.23$, $p<0.0005$. It is extremely unlikely that
the variables are simultaneously 0. To this it may be added $R^2 = 0.57$.

What then of the effect of polygyny controlling for GDP? Births per
one thousand go up, as per the regression coefficient ($b = 4.690576$) and
the apparent rejection of the two-tailed statistical test ($p<0.0005$).

The scatter of points in Figure 3.3 suggests that "Births, Women Aged
15–19" in countries with higher degrees of polygyny are also on average
more substantial, and this too is what is to be expected of the line of best
fit, and also from the relative tightness of the confidence interval.

To compile multivariate evidence of the effect of polygyny, a multiple regression controlling for GDP was performed. The fit statistic
with $F\ (2,\ 134) = 41.57$ indicates that the variables are not jointly 0,
at a high level of significance ($p<0.0005$). There is more evidence of an
association in the form of the squared correlation coefficient, namely,
$R^2 = 0.38$.

This regression indicates the separate effect of polygyny, with a large
and positive coefficient estimated as $b = 16.885980$, with estimated standard

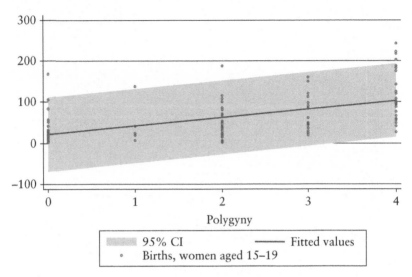

Figure 3.3. Scatterplot, Line of Best Fit, and Confidence Intervals for Births, Women Aged 15–19, by Polygyny

Note: A bivariate regression was used to calculate the line of best fit while CI is the uncertainty of prediction.

error of 2.724238, and a *p*-value beyond what is conventionally required for rejection of the null hypothesis ($p<0.0005$).

Polygyny also exerts an effect on children's welfare. Girls are less likely to receive an education in primary or secondary school as polygyny becomes more frequent. The same holds true for boys. Boys are less likely to receive either primary or secondary school education in polygynous societies than are boys raised in monogamous societies.

The rates of primary enrollment of girls in school are shown in Table 3.2 and Figure 3.4. Figure 3.4 suggests that in countries that have lower primary enrollments of girls, polygyny is more frequent, on average. This is shown by the scatter of data and the line of best fit. The confidence interval suggests confidence in the predictions.

A two-variable multiple regression fits the outcome variable reasonably well. Indeed, F (2, 156) = 11.11, $p<0.0005$, and R^2 = 0.12. As evinced by Figure 3.4, the coefficient linking polygyny to primary enrollment for girls is negative (b = –4.454723) and statistically significant ($p<0.0005$), as anticipated. This means that in polygynous countries, girls are less likely to attend primary schools.

TABLE 3.2. Effect of Polygyny and GDP on Births, Women Aged 15–19, and Female Enrollment, Primary

Variable	Births, Women Aged 15–19			Primary Enrollment for Women		
	Coefficient	S.E.	*p*-value	Coefficient	S.E.	*p*-value
Polygyny	16.885980	2.724238	<0.0005	–4.454723	1.018081	<0.0005
GDP	–0.000865	0.000265	<0.001	0.000001	0.000102	>.992
N		137			159	
		$F_{(2, 134)} = 41.57, p<0.0005$			$F_{(2, 156)} = 11.11, p<0.0005$	
R^2		0.38			0.12	

Notes: Coefficients, associated standard errors, *p*-values, and fit statistics from ols regressions with births (15–19) and female enrollment (primary) as dependent variables and polygyny and GDP in each of the regressions as independent variables.

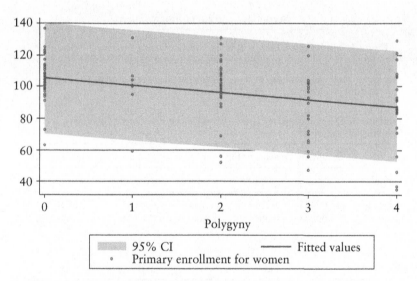

Figure 3.4. Scatterplot, Line of Best Fit, and Confidence Intervals for Primary Enrollment for Women by Polygyny

Note: A bivariate regression was used to calculate the line of best fit while CI is the uncertainty of prediction.

The fifth outcome variable, secondary enrollment of girls in school, behaves in response to polygyny in the same way as that for primary enrollment. Figure 3.5 displays this, composed as it is with the scatter, the slope estimate, and the confidence interval.

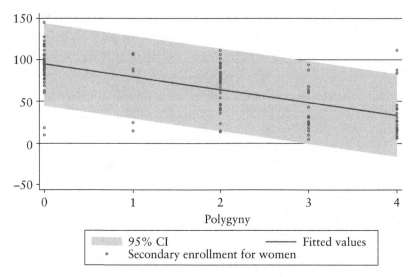

Figure 3.5. Scatterplot, Line of Best Fit, and Confidence Intervals for Secondary Enrollment for Women by Polygyny

Note: A bivariate regression was used to calculate the line of best fit while CI is the uncertainty of prediction.

TABLE 3.3. Effect of Polygyny and GDP on Female Enrollment, Secondary, and Male Enrollment, Primary

| Variable | Secondary Enrollment for Women | | | Primary Enrollment for Men | | |
	Coefficient	S.E.	*p*-value	Coefficient	S.E.	*p*-value
Polygyny	−12.064350	1.291731	<0.0005	−7.429632	3.675072	<0.045
GDP	0.000861	0.000129	<0.0005	−0.000531	0.000367	>0.151
N		158			159	
	F (2, 155) = 102.90, *p*<0.0005			F (2, 159) = 2.32, *p*<0.1012		
R²		0.57			0.03	

Notes: Coefficients, associated standard errors, *p*-values, and fit statistics from ols regressions with female enrollment (secondary) and male enrollment (primary) as dependent variables and polygyny and GDP in each of the regressions as independent variables.

The fit is better, however. Table 3.3 contains the results. F (2, 155) = 102.90, *p*<0.0005, and R² = 0.57. Moreover, it can be seen that secondary enrollment of girls declines as polygyny becomes more frequent (β = −12.064350), and in a statistically significant way (*p*<0.0005).

What then of the sixth outcome variable and the seventh, namely, the degree of primary and secondary enrollment for boys in school? In both cases, seen in Figures 3.6 and 3.7, enrollment for boys appears structured

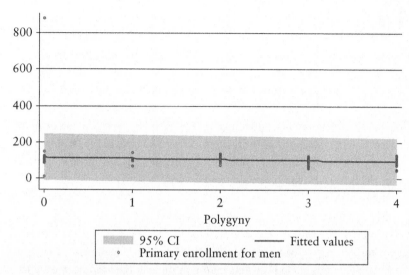

Figure 3.6. Scatterplot, Line of Best Fit, and Confidence Intervals for Primary Enrollment for Men by Polygyny

Note: A bivariate regression was used to calculate the line of best fit while CI is the uncertainty of prediction.

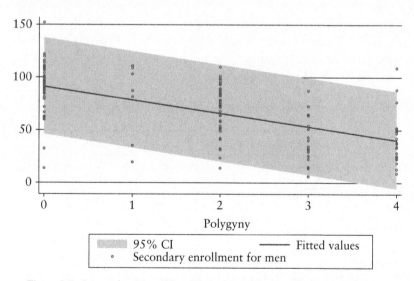

Figure 3.7. Scatterplot, Line of Best Fit, and Confidence Intervals for Secondary Enrollment for Men by Polygyny

Note: A bivariate regression was used to calculate the line of best fit while CI is the uncertainty of prediction.

at least partially by polygyny. The slope of line of best fit is negative in both cases: lower enrollments of boys in primary or secondary institutions are on average occurring in countries with higher levels of polygyny.

While these figures are suggestive, multiple regression is ultimately necessary to untangle the question of the role of polygyny for these outcome variables, and the technique for both outcome variables confirms how polygyny affects them, controlling for GDP. To begin with, for primary education the fit statistics—$F (2, 159) = 2.32$, $p<0.1012$, $R^2 = 0.03$—suggest a relationship between GDP and/or polygyny and primary education for boys. Moreover, the slope ($\beta = -7.429632$) is statistically significant ($p<0.045$).

Moving to secondary enrollment, Table 3.4 shows a good fitting equation: $F (2, 155) = 94.90$, $p<0.0005$, $R^2 = 0.55$, indeed far more so than for primary enrollment. Moreover, secondary enrollment of boys in more polygynous societies is less common on average as indicated by the regression coefficient ($\beta = -9.722135$) and the two-tailed statistical test ($p<0.0005$).

Increased polygyny also heightens the difference in the occurrence of HIV infection between women and men; women become more likely relative to men to suffer from HIV as polygyny becomes more common. The differences in HIV rates, as displayed by Figure 3.8, are loosely driven by polygyny: the line of best fit to the scatter cloud notes that the difference between HIV rates between women and men becomes larger, on average, in countries more beset by polygyny.

TABLE 3.4. Effect of Polygyny and GDP on Male Enrollment, Secondary, and HIV (Difference)

Variable	Secondary Enrollment for Men			HIV		
	Coefficient	S.E.	p-value	Coefficient	S.E.	p-value
Polygyny	−9.722135	1.165776	<0.0005	0.377731	0.201288	<0.064
GDP	0.000829	0.000117	<0.0005	−0.000021	0.000020	>0.314
N		158			94	
	$F (2, 155) = 94.90$, $p<0.0005$			$F (2, 91) = 4.85$, $p<0.01$		
R^2		0.55			0.10	

Notes: Coefficients, associated standard errors, p-values, and fit statistics from ols regressions with male enrollment (secondary) and HIV (difference between women and men) as dependent variables and polygyny and GDP in each of the regressions as independent variables.

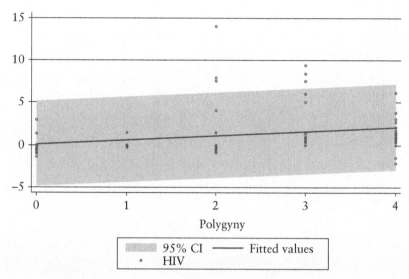

Figure 3.8. Scatterplot, Line of Best Fit, and Confidence Intervals for HIV by Polygyny

Note: A bivariate regression was used to calculate the line of best fit while CI is the uncertainty of prediction.

The fit statistics for the multiple regression indicate a joint or possible one variable relationship is at stake: F (2, 91) = 4.85, $p<0.01$, $R^2 = 0.10$; it should be noted that the estimated variance explained is not particularly impressive.

The relationship between the difference in HIV rates and polygyny survives a multiple regression analysis (β = 0.377731) and the two-tailed statistical test ($p<0.064$). To be sure, the latter misses the 0.05 level, but it should be added that a one-tailed test is reasonable given the expected direction of the relationship, and this being the case, the multiple regression coefficient is significant at conventional levels ($p<0.032$).

Women in polygynous countries are more likely to marry at a younger age than women in countries where polygyny is less frequent. The scatter of points in Figure 3.9 shows that female marriage age in countries with higher degrees of polygyny is on average lower, and the line of best fit reinforces this. The confidence interval adheres at a reasonable level about the regression line.

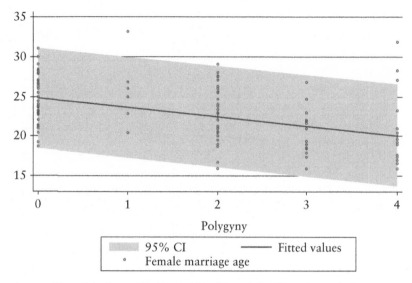

Figure 3.9. Scatterplot, Line of Best Fit, and Confidence Intervals for Female Marriage Age by Polygyny

Note: A bivariate regression was used to calculate the line of best fit while CI is the uncertainty of prediction.

TABLE 3.5. Effect of Polygyny and GDP on Female Marriage Age and Maternal Mortality

	Female Marriage Age			Maternal Mortality		
Variable	Coefficient	S.E.	*p*-value	Coefficient	S.E.	*p*-value
Polygyny	–0.751378	0.162937	<0.0005	131.537200	19.492820	<0.0005
GDP	0.000114	0.000117	<0.0005	–0.007075	0.002008	<0.0005
N		153			170	
	F (2, 153) = 54.84, *p*<0.0005			F (2, 167) = 42.83, *p*<0.0005		
R^2		0.42			0.34	

Notes: Coefficients, associated standard errors, *p*-values, and fit statistics from ols regressions with female marriage age and maternal mortality as dependent variables and polygyny and GDP in each of the regressions as independent variables.

Confirming demonstration of the effect of polygyny comes in the form of a multiple regression controlling for GDP. This has three parts. First, the fit statistic indicates that the variables are not jointly 0: F (2, 153) = 54.84, *p*<0.0005. Second, there is more evidence of an association, namely,

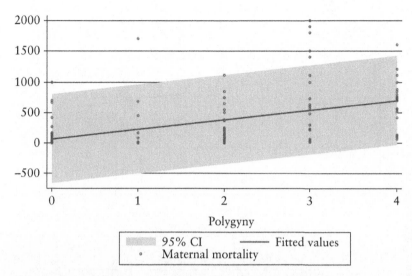

Figure 3.10. Scatterplot, Line of Best Fit, and Confidence Intervals for Maternal Mortality by Polygyny

Note: A bivariate regression was used to calculate the line of best fit while CI is the uncertainty of prediction.

$R^2 = 0.42$, the squared correlation coefficient. Third, the slope coefficient is negative ($\beta = -0.751378$). There can be little statistical doubt the null hypothesis is false ($p<0.0005$).

Women are more likely to die in childbirth as countries become more polygynous. The scatter of points in Figure 3.10, and the accompanying line of best fit and the confidence interval, is consistent with the hypothesis that as polygyny gets more extensive so does maternal mortality, defined as the number of women who died in childbirth per one hundred thousand live births.

A multiple regression affirms that the coefficients linking polygyny and GDP to maternal mortality are not jointly zero—$F_{(2, 167)} = 42.83$, $p<0.0005$, $R^2 = 0.34$—meaning that both GDP and polygyny, or one of these, contribute to maternal mortality. Multiple regression with GDP as a control produces results reinforcing what is suggested by the bivariate regression.

Polygyny has a separate role to play. Its corresponding coefficient is estimated as ($\beta = 131.537200$), with estimated standard error of 19.492820,

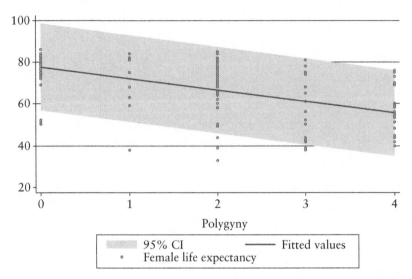

Figure 3.11. Scatterplot, Line of Best Fit, and Confidence Intervals for Female Life Expectancy by Polygyny

Note: A bivariate regression was used to calculate the line of best fit while CI is the uncertainty of prediction.

and a *p*-value beyond what is conventionally required for rejection of the null hypothesis ($p<0.0005$).

Longevity is also affected by polygyny. Life expectancy taps the average age at which women in a given country die. Polygyny and female life expectancy are inversely linked: more polygynous countries experience lower life expectancy for females. In other words, women in more polygynous countries die at a younger age on average, likely at least partly because they are more likely to die in childbirth as noted above. Figure 3.11 portrays in two-space the relationship between female life expectancy and polygyny and the according line of best fit, surrounded on either side by the confidence interval. In polygynous societies female life expectancy is lower than in societies without it.

It can be seen from Table 3.6 that a multiple regression with polygyny and GDP as predictors fares well: $F_{(2, 153)} = 74.28$, $p<0.0005$, $R^2 = 0.47$. The same may be said for polygyny considered on its own, GDP serving as a control. The coefficient is negative ($\beta = -4.479878$), and a high degree of confidence can be expressed in the rejection of the null hypothesis ($p<0.0005$).

TABLE 3.6. The Effect of Polygyny and GDP on Female Life Expectancy

Variable	Female Life Expectancy		
	Coefficient	S.E.	*p*-value
Polygyny	–4.479878	0.535178	<0.0005
GDP	0.000293	0.000055	<0.0005
N		153	
	F (2, 153) = 74.28, *p*<0.0005		
R^2		0.47	

Notes: Coefficients, associated standard errors, *p*-values, and fit statistics with female life expectancy as a dependent variable and polygyny and GDP in the regression as independent variables.

Ordered logistic regression was used to estimate the relationship between the following dependent variables and polygyny, with GDP used in all analyses as a control: sex trafficking; female genital mutilation (FGM); domestic violence (DVS); and inequity in family law. From a statistical standpoint, this technique has many advantages over ordinary least squares regression when the dependent variable is comprised of a limited number of ordered, unevenly spaced categories.

Sex trafficking increases in more polygynous countries. This variable divides countries into five categories, based on their degree of compliance with the Trafficking Persons Act of 2000. The lowest signifies that there are laws against sex trafficking, while the highest means that sex trafficking is permitted and the country is not in compliance with the law. In the current analysis, the five-point scale in the WomanStats database was collapsed into four categories because there were not a sufficient number of observations in two of the categories. Specifically, we collapsed the lowest two categories, since only one country fit into the lowest category. When this happens, the coefficients cannot be properly estimated, so this is standard practice in such cases. Table 3.7 displays the results of a proposed model of predictors consisting of polygyny and GDP. The likelihood ratio test for the model produces beta 2 (3) = 64.96, which yields *p*<0.0005. Consequently, it is very unlikely that the coefficients linking our independent variables to sex trafficking are both 0. The pseudo-R^2 = 0.17 suggests a relationship, though the degree cannot be quantified statistically.

TABLE 3.7. Effects of Polygyny and GDP on Sex Trafficking and FGM

	Sex Trafficking			FGM		
Variable	Odds Ratio	S.E.	p-value	Odds Ratio	S.E.	p-value
Polygyny	1.251951	0.141874	<0.047	3.763611	0.944152	<0.0005
GDP	0.999901	0.000018	<0.0005	1.000018	0.000019	>.365
N		154			74	
LR X2(3)		64.96, p<0.0005			48.53, p<0.0005	
Pseudo-R²		0.17			0.31	

Notes: Coefficients, associated standard errors, p-values, and fit statistics from two separate ordinal logistic regressions with sex trafficking and FGM, respectively, as dependent variables and in each ordinal logistic regression polygyny and GDP as independent variables. Odds ratios indicate how the odds of the dependent variable change in response to shifts in an independent variable.

A two-tailed test for the hypothesis that polygyny has no effect on sex trafficking may be rejected using a standard level of significance ($p<0.047$). One demonstration of the effect of polygyny is via the odds ratio: a movement from one level of polygyny to one immediately subsequent to it increases the odds of being in the uppermost category of the ordered, discrete sex trafficking scale versus the other categories by a factor of 1.25 times, GDP controlled.

Envisioning the effect of polygyny on sex trafficking via an odds ratio can be supplemented with a consideration of the effect of polygyny on predicted probabilities associated with categories of sex trafficking. In calculating the degree of association, though, it needs emphasizing that while odds ratios do not turn on the values of polygyny or GDP—where they are fixed, in particular—the predicted probabilities for sex trafficking must be calculated for levels of polygyny and some fixed value for GDP.

This is due to the fact that the probabilities associated with categories of the dependent variables are nonlinear expressions of the independent variables: the interpretation of the effect of polygyny for one (fixed) value of GDP may be somewhat different than that for another, whereas the odds ratio associated with a shift from one level of polygyny to the one immediately following is the same regardless of whether one starts with, say, polygyny=2 or polygyny=3.

However, the same is not true when the matter turns to predicted probabilities for sex trafficking, or any of our other ordinal dependent

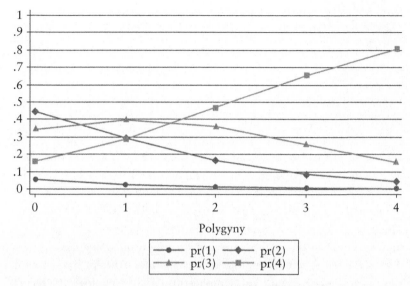

Figure 3.12. Effect of Polygyny on the Predicted Probabilities of Categories of Family Law

Note: Each line represents how the predicted probabilities of a category of family law alter in response to changes in polygyny.

variables. Even so, while caution must be exercised, it is still the case that a portrait of predicted probabilities has a substantive and visual appeal, particularly when accompanied by a figure plotting the effects.

Such is the case with Figure 3.12. The y-axis ranges from 0 to 1, as expected. The x-axis is polygyny, with graphically represented steps of 1 from 0 to 4, also expected. What do the lines represent? How can they be interpreted?

For a particular category, say sex trafficking=4, the lines trace the effect of polygyny from one level to another, and further, across its range: how a change, say, from polygyny=2 to polygyny=3 alters the predicted probabilities of sex trafficking when the value of sex trafficking is 4.

Notice also that the slopes linking various categories step by step through the range of polygyny are not identical. For instance, when sex trafficking=1 (p=1), its associated predicted probabilities generally go down when polygyny goes down, while the general movement of predicted probabilities when sex trafficking=4 goes up as polygyny becomes more common. What this means, in fact, is that as polygyny becomes more frequent, trafficking becomes more prevalent and women more victimized. As signaled by the figure, the leap in predicted probabilities for this value of trafficking is impressive, particularly since GDP is controlled at its median value, a good choice given that this is a measure of central tendency.

FGM, sometimes referred to as "female cutting," also increases as countries become more polygynous. This practice exerts a detrimental effect on women's health because it can affect subsequent bladder, bowel, and childbirth processes, particularly if it is badly done or conducted under unsanitary conditions, as often occurs. This practice is often referred to as "female circumcision," but this term represents a clear misnomer and euphemism. As Toubia writes in the *New England Journal of Medicine*: "The mildest form, clitoridectomy, is anatomically equivalent to amputation of the penis. Under the conditions in which most procedures take place, female circumcision constitutes a health hazard with short- and long-term physical complications and psychological effects" (1994, 3).

In our analysis, the highest category includes countries where more than 10 percent, and sometimes upwards of 50 percent, of women have sustained such cutting. FGM is divided by countries into five categories and then collapsed into three for purposes of the analysis because of the small number of cases for particular values of the variable.

The number of cases here is comparatively small, suggesting perhaps that caution is warranted in interpreting the results. But such is not written in stone; alternatively, it might be speculated that countries with the highest levels of FGM do not report this, perhaps looking away, perhaps encouraging it, the impact of this being a suppressor effect—the relationship might look even stronger were data available for all countries.

This said, the likelihood ratio test for our model of two variables is distributed beta 2 (3) = 48.53, which yields $p<0.0005$. So we can reject at conventional levels the hypothesis of a joint, null relationship between FGM and our two independent variables.

The pseudo-R^2 = 0.31 is the highest so far seen. A linkage between polygyny and FGM is confirmed statistically with a very high degree of significance ($p<0.0005$). This magnitude is especially impressive and is confirmed by the shape of the lines in Figure 3.13. At its most extreme, FGM has predicted probabilities that move almost in lockstep with polygyny.

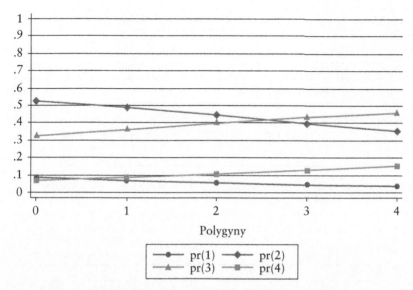

Figure 3.13. Effect of Polygyny on the Predicted Probabilities of Categories of Sex Trafficking

Note: Each line represents how the predicted probabilities of a category of family law alter in response to changes in polygyny.

Of critical importance is the question of whether polygyny helps cause violence toward women. To answer this question, an omnibus measure of DVS was employed, one that incorporates DVS, rape, marital rape, and honor killings, as well as the extent and strength of the enforcement of the laws prohibiting these crimes in any given state. And indeed, as confirmed in Table 3.8 and Figure 3.14, polygynous countries contain more DVS against women. Table 3.8 shows the likelihood ratio test for our model of two variables is distributed beta 2 (3) = 76.03, which yields $p<0.0005$. So we can reject at conventional levels the hypothesis of a joint, null relationship between DVS and our two independent variables. A supplementary suggestion of a relationship comes courtesy of the pseudo-R^2 = 0.19.

Our test statistic suggests that one or both of our variables drive DVS, so what then of the effect of polygyny? A linkage between polygyny and DVS is confirmed statistically with a very high degree of significance ($p<0.001$). The odds ratio may be interpreted by assessing how moving polygyny by one unit upward shifts the odds of being in the uppermost category of the ordered, discrete DVS scale versus the other categories of

TABLE 3.8. Effects of Polygyny and GDP on DVS and Inequity

	DVS			Inequity		
Variable	Odds Ratio	S.E.	p-value	Odds Ratio	S.E.	p-value
Polygyny	1.466550	0.163000	<0.001	3.059176	0.423937	<0.0005
GDP	0.999916	0.000015	<0.0005	0.999935	0.000014	<0.0005
N		168			170	
LR X2(3)		76.03, p<0.0005			139.07, p<0.0005	
Pseudo-R²		0.19			0.27	

Coefficients, associated standard errors, p-values, and fit statistics from two separate ordinal logistic regressions with FGM and inequity, respectively, as dependent variables and in each case polygyny and GDP as independent variables.

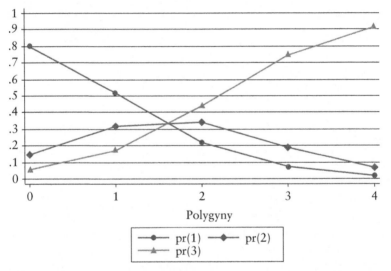

Figure 3.14. Effect of Polygyny on the Predicted Probabilities of Categories of FGM

Note: Each line represents how the predicted probabilities of a category of family law alter in response to changes in polygyny.

DVS. Indeed, the odds increase by 1.47 times, GDP controlled. For the value of GDP we have chosen, it can be seen that DVS at its worst expression p(4), and as expressed in terms of predicted probabilities, goes up as considered across the range of polygyny (Figure 3.14). There is also a dramatic on-balance shift for the category of DVS=2 (p=2).

Polygyny also affects the treatment of men and women before the law. Differences in the legal treatment of women versus men become greater, to the detriment of women, in more polygynous societies. We refer to this variable as inequity. Inequity measures the degree of equal treatment of men and women before the law. More particularly, inequity is defined as the relative standing of men and women under law, indexed on an ordinal scale. At the low end are countries where the legal age of marriage is eighteen or higher, where women may choose their spouse, where divorce is possible, where both partners are treated equitably by law, where abortion is permitted, and where women may inherit property. Countries at the high end permit marriage at younger than eighteen years of age (e.g., have laws that permit girls aged twelve or less to be married) and have laws more restrictive to women's rights on the other facets of this omnibus measure. Table 3.8 contains the results.

Our two-variable model performs well, as expressed by a likelihood ratio test, with a distribution beta 2 (3) = 139.07, which yields $p<0.0005$. So we can reject at conventional levels the hypothesis of a joint, null relationship between inequity and our two independent variables. As noted and absent a distribution, the pseudo-R^2 = 0.27 conveys the same information as the likelihood ratio statistic.

More evidence for the hypothesis that polygyny matters with regard to inequity comes in the form of a two-tailed statistical test of the null hypothesis that it does not ($p<0.0005$). The accompanying information about predicted probabilities, displayed in Figure 3.15, is difficult to summarize and is perhaps our most notable manifestation of nonlinearities. We observe what we would expect: dips on balance when inequity manifests in its greatest form as polygyny turns from its lowest to its greatest amount, and the reverse being so when polygyny travels from its greatest to its lowest, driving as it does inequity at its lowest level.

Polygyny also has effects that extend beyond the outcome variables already considered. Polygyny can also exert effects on various aspects of domestic and international politics for a given nation-state. First, to the extent that junior boys who have been excised from polygynous communities become wards of the state, the cost of educating, socializing, housing, feeding, and job training for them gets transferred from the family to taxpayers. Second, to the extent that secondary wives can obtain aid from the state under laws designed to help women with dependent children without men, since polygynous unions are sometimes not recognized by

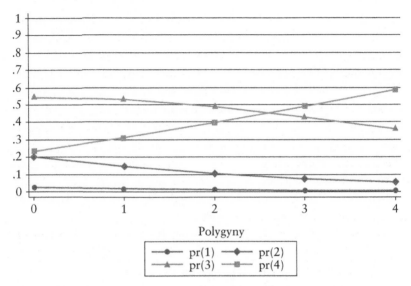

Figure 3.15. Effect of Polygyny on the Predicted Probabilities of Categories of DVS

Note: Each line represents how the predicted probabilities of a category of family law alter in response to changes in polygyny.

the state, especially in more Western countries, financial costs for such support can escalate as well.

Moreover, the effects of polygyny on the nation-state can be quantified along certain dimensions. States with higher rates of polygyny spend more money per capita on defense, particularly on arms expenditures for weapons.

More specifically, we test whether defense expenditures have a partial foundation in polygyny. Defense expenditures are surely a crucial foreign policy stance, an orientation toward the outside world and perhaps an indication of the inner workings of policy elites. So polygyny is examined here for the extent to which it can exert influential impacts beyond the private and domestic spheres.

We further investigate whether states with high levels of polygyny concurrently have low degrees of freedom, the former being a cause of the latter, and the latter a crucial measure of the internal workings of the state and the quality of life for all citizens.

We begin with defense expenditures. SIPRI has collected data about defense expenditures per capita. A particular advantage of this measure,

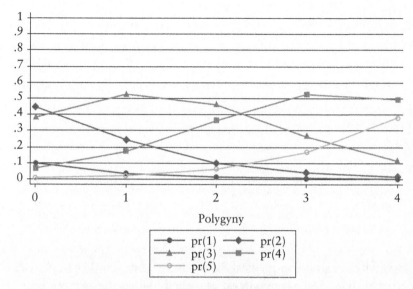

Figure 3.16. Effect of Polygyny on the Predicted Probabilities of
Categories of Inequity

Note: Each line represents how the predicted probabilities of a category of family law alter
in response to changes in polygyny.

aside from its being well respected and widely used, is that the unit of
analysis is the state, permitting what we have already done, particularly a comparison of states with lower versus higher levels of polygyny
with states that have lower or higher levels of outcomes negative toward
women, on average. Our question is whether this variable is related to
polygyny.

Figure 3.16, complete with the scatter of data, the line of best fit, and
the confidence interval, is consistent with the interpretation that states
with higher amounts of per capita defense expenditures are more likely on
average to have higher degrees of polygyny. Table 3.9 confirms this. The
fit statistic confirms this marginally $F (2, 91) = 2.73$, $p<0.0687$, and the
squared correlation coefficient is $R^2 = 0.22$. The coefficient is 0.228663 and
is statistically significant at conventional levels ($p<0.025$). We can conclude
from this that states with higher expenditures are, on average, more likely
to have higher degrees of polygyny as well. This is as we anticipated.

Polygyny also influences the degree of rights and freedoms experienced
by citizens in a given country. Specifically, states with higher rates of

TABLE 3.9. Effects of Polygyny and GDP on Defense Expenditures and Freedom

	SIPRI			Freedom		
Variable	Coefficient	S.E.	p-value	Odds Ratio	S.E.	p-value
Polygyny	0.228663	0.100777	<0.025	0.682354	0.076193	<0.001
GDP	0.000004	0.000010	>0.68	1.000076	0.000020	<0.0005
N		137			166	
	F (2, 91) = 2.73, p<0.0687			LR X2(2) = 52.28, p<0.0005		
	R^2 = 0.22			Pseudo-R^2 = 0.1463		

Notes: Coefficients, associated standard errors, *p*-values, and fit statistics from one ols regression (defense expenditures) and one ordinal logistic regression (freedom). The ordinary least squares regression and the ordinal least squares regression both employ the same independent variables, viz., polygyny and GDP. Still, the interpretation of the coefficient for polygyny in the ordinary least squares regression (as so for GDP) is not the same as that for the odds ratio for polygyny (as so for GDP).

polygyny display fewer political rights and civil liberties than those with less polygyny. To be sure, a good deal about the liberties women enjoy, and the ones stripped from them because of their gender, can easily be inferred using data from the project. But here the consideration is liberties more generally construed within society at large, those experienced by both men and women, and there is no measured analog for that in the WomanStats Project database. On the other hand, Freedom House has an excellent, well-thought-of omnibus measure, described as "freedom in world historical rankings." A particular advantage of this measure is that the unit of analysis is the state, permitting what we have already done, particularly a comparison of states with lower versus higher levels of polygyny with states that have lower or higher levels of outcomes negative toward citizens, on average.

Summarizing the results of the ordered logistic regression, it can be seen from Table 3.9, beta 2 (2) = 52.28, *p*<0.0005. Thus we can dispense with the null hypothesis that there is jointly no effect of the predictors of the measured level of freedom. It is also the case that polygyny survives as an influence, GDP controlled (*p*<0.0005). Though elsewhere not to be as diagnostic in the same ways as the likelihood ratio statistics, the pseudo-R^2 = 0.1463 is suggestive of relationship between at least one of the variables and freedom.

The odds ratio is 0.682354 and statistically significant (*p*<0.001) meaning that moving one category upward in polygyny lowers by 0.682354

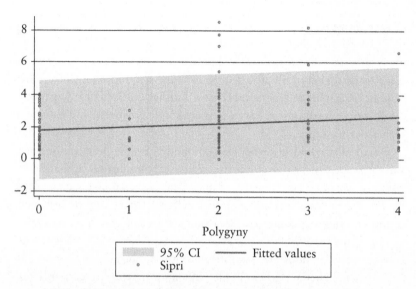

Figure 3.17. Scatterplot, Line of Best Fit, and Confidence Intervals for
Sipri by Polygyny

Note: A bivariate regression was used to calculate the line of best fit while CI is the
uncertainty of prediction.

times that a country will be free as opposed to the two (ordered) alternative. The final figure visually shows how, when GDP is controlled for at
its median, changes in polygyny affect the level of freedom of a state. As
an example, look at the predicted probabilities for a state as "not free."
These probabilities, when looked at when polygyny is absent, are lower
than the predicted probabilities when at least 25 percent of women are
captured by polygyny.

Discussion and Conclusions

Examining over 170 countries around the world, we find that polygynous
structures increase violence toward women and children, decrease civil
rights and political liberties in the state more broadly, and increase the
allocation of resources in society toward weapons procurement as well.
Polygyny exerts economic, physical, and political consequences for societies in which such practices remain prevalent. For example, Kanazawa

(2001) shows early menarche in polygynous countries, and unrelated work has shown that early sexual trauma, common in polygyny where many girls are forced into early marriage to much older, abusive men, leads to increased morbidity, decline in longevity, and intergenerational transfer of changes in genetic expression. Further, children of young mothers do worse in education, have worse economic prospects, and remain at higher risk for crime.

Our results could in theory be confounded by the presence of other variables not considered in our analysis, such as religious affiliation or political system. The strengths of statistical association might also be modified by taking into account sociocultural similarities or historical continuities among countries. Controlling for such variables represents an important analytical challenge that has been solved when relationships between sample points are linguistic or cultural, but not for countries as a whole since they include multiple populations. Data are currently not available to analyze by distinct cultural units. Future research may be able to test such hypotheses when further data become available. Furthermore, it is possible that causation can go in both directions. For example, female-biased mortality arising from violence toward women could lead to polygyny being favored.

Nevertheless, the consistency and strength of our findings across multiple independent measures of violence, together with their conformity to a well-supported anthropological theory about the impact of polygyny on the propensity for male violence, are clearly suggestive. In view of the importance of recognizing sources of violence that can be modified by appropriate legislative action, we believe our results warrant further intense investigation. Moreover, policymakers would have to change multiple laws across multiple domains to exert as much of an effect on these negative outcomes toward women and children as could be accomplished by the abolition of polygyny. We conclude that the evidence in favor of the role of polygyny is sufficiently strong that efforts should be made to understand more clearly the contexts in which, and the mechanisms by which, polygyny fosters local and institutional violence toward women and children, as well as its role in undergirding support for the suppression of political rights and civil liberties. In addition, polygyny exerts its effects on violence against women independent of the effects of sex ratio alone, so the social, cultural, and institutional practices that support its existence manifest an impact that goes beyond merely increasing the number of unmarried men in society.

Our data also show that increased GDP is generally associated with women having greater freedom from violence. We suggest that wealthier countries may have more resources, and possibly more willingness to devote such resources, to more accurate collection of data on many aspects of society, including the treatment of women and children. We also suspect that as income rises, societies have increased wherewithal to treat women and children better. Possible explanations include women having more power because they generate a higher percentage of the wealth, allowing them to be less economically dependent on men. In addition, wealthier societies might monitor conformity to the law more accurately, thanks to their greater resources. However, the problem of violence against women is not obviated by increasing wealth alone, as attested by the fact that many wealthy countries continue to suffer high rates of violence against women, including DVS, rape, and murder. Poverty, while clearly important, represents only part of the problem generating violence against women. Polygyny constitutes an additional important piece of the puzzle. As long as this kind of family structure continues its legitimate status throughout much of the world, its consequences will continue to exert independent effects on the violent outcomes of concern. In other words, polygyny as well as poverty will have to be tackled before societies can gain a firm grasp on the challenge of reducing or eliminating violence against women and children within them.

More than simply increasing the number of men unable to find mates, polygynous practices also encourage control over women in many areas of social and political life, a practice required in order to maintain control over reproductive access. This analysis demonstrates that such control often devolves into systematic practices of violence against women and children. In this way, polygyny may represent a more sensitive measure of patriarchy than sex ratio, since sex ratio includes women outside reproductive age. This age structure distribution may be particularly important with regard to older women; it may not matter much if there are a lot of old women compared to old men in terms of the impact of sex ratio on violence against women, but it may matter a great deal if most younger women are engaged in polygynous unions.

Polygyny appears to constitute a sizeable and independent piece of the puzzle explaining the emergence of violence directed at women and children. In addition, the institutions necessary to keep it in place may help explain some of the patterns of repression across the globe. This is a practice that will not necessarily be easily changed. One solution offered to the problem of polygyny as a source of violence toward women might be to increase female social emancipation through education. Yet Lesthaeghe et al. (1994) found that increasing female literacy did not lead to a decline in polygyny rates, at least in sub-Saharan Africa. Reading does not help if the only information one encounters merely reconfirms preexisting beliefs. As long as male control of reading material is maintained, female literacy alone cannot begin to shift patterns of patriarchal control until women begin to possess the financial, economic, and social foundations of independence as well.

For those interested in human rights, the relationship between polygyny and violence against women should be particularly alarming. Indeed, an irony emerges from our analysis: conventional attempts to empower women in polygynous culture can be expected to make matters worse because they will increase the hostility felt by many men toward the women and the cultural values that advocate for female emancipation. We do not conclude that such efforts, including advocacy of women's rights and education of both sexes, should be discontinued. But the inherent obstacles that they face should be appreciated. The cultural and political diversity of polygynous cultures creates many different opportunities for sensitively designed efforts to work, even if the emancipation of women can be predicted to encounter continuing resistance in various regions, including especially those culturally dominated by polygyny. It is important to remain aware of the fact that areas where such practices are common may prove more impervious to an improvement in women's rights than areas where such practices are less frequent.

After all, polygyny does not necessarily stem from women's being uneducated. If it is rooted in a local socioeconomic system, economics rather than ideas may need to change in order to alter the incentives sustaining its practice. Empowering women alone is not enough. If the underlying causes of the male domination of the rights of reproduction remain unchanged, female emancipation will be limited. Such efforts therefore need to be complemented with strategies that address the deep causes of patriarchy, including polygynous family structures.

We do not intend here to assume that all practices that most Westerners see as repressive of women need to be changed, such as the wearing of the veil. But neither do we intend to embrace cultural relativism to the disservice of basic human rights and peaceful coexistence. Rather, we take note of Abu-Lughod's (2002) directive to recognize the historical and economic forces that engendered this reality and work to transform it within the context of a universal responsibility to mitigate injustice and prevent harm and injury to all humans, while respecting genuine cultural preferences that do not impinge on basic human rights. With this in mind, we offer two observations.

The urban explosion of young, unmarried men could produce great social and political volatility. High-status men may still be able to secure lots of wives, and low-status men will still not be able to garner any wives, but since inevitably there will be more of the latter than the former, it becomes possible to rally the low-status males to overturn the system through sheer numbers. Establishing alliances with these disenfranchised men can serve only to encourage the transition that would be best for individual women and society alike. These men may be facilitated in this transition by women who may prefer not sharing a husband, which admittedly may not encompass all women.

A bigger question concerns polygyny. Polygynous cultures where men control women and their reproduction support and encourage violence both within these societies as well as outside of them. Polygynous cultures leave many young, lower-class men without sexual partners and prone toward violence. They also provide men who have daughters with a certain amount of wealth and status that result from their control over a scarce resource. Elaborate cultures and hierarchies rest on this control over women forced into passivity.

Cultural values that favor female emancipation, which threatens to replace passive participants with independent women, can frighten and enrage men in areas where control and domination of the productive and reproductive capacities of women embody an important source of power. In the face of their own poverty and unemployment, men who lose control over women may feel that they are left with nothing of value. Such a prospect renders these men particularly dangerous because they have nothing to lose in fighting a force that threatens their only status and prospects for reproduction. As long as polygynous marital practices offer opportunities for such men to use their control of women for their own personal power, wealth, and status, any threat to such a system will spawn rage and violence in response. Such systems will leave large numbers of poor men without women.

History suggests two sets of options that governments confronted with too many men have engaged to try to deal with this problem (Hudson and den Boer 2002). They can try policies that reduce the number of men, either through violence or by exporting them to other countries as missionaries or mercenaries. Or they can try to increase the number of women, by importing brides or by reducing processes such as sex-selective abortion, female infanticide, female death in childbirth, and early childhood death of girls. But these are stop-gap measures. As long as polygyny persists, countries run a high risk of violence—which may or may not be exported beyond their borders. Only when these structures no longer present an opportunity for such men to benefit from their dominance of women will women's emancipation no longer present a fundamental threat to these cultures.

It may be time, therefore, for human rights advocates to consider a campaign to attempt to ban polygyny. The risk is that this would be seen as one more attempt to impose Western values on the developing world in ways that remain antithetical to their traditional cultural values. But just as the developing world might point to the seeds of terrorism in Western economic and political injustice, so too can the developed world discover some of the sources of violence and repression in the social injustice inherent in polygyny. Abolishing polygyny and encouraging female emancipation is a formula for a safer world. By prohibiting polygyny, we reduce social inequities, violence toward women and children, and the proliferation of single men and the violence they perpetuate, as well as increase political rights and civil liberties for all.

References

Abu-Lughod, Lila. 2002. "Do Muslim Women Really Need Saving? Anthropological Reflections on Cultural Relativism and Its Others." *American Anthropologist* 104:783–90.

Courtwright, David T. 1996. *Violent Land: Single Men and Social Disorder from the Frontier to the Inner City.* Cambridge, MA: Harvard University Press.

Daly, Martin, and Margo Wilson. 1999. "Darwinism and the Roots of Machismo." *Scientific American* 10:8–14.

Drèze, Jean, and Reetika Khera. 2000. "Crime, Gender, and Society in India: Insights from Homicide Data." *Population and Development Review* 26:335–52.

Fallers, Lloyd, and Margaret Fallers. 1976. "Sex Roles in Edremit." In *Mediterranean Family Structures,* edited by J. G. Peristiany, 243–60. Cambridge: Cambridge University Press.

Gray, Peter B., Sonya M. Kahlenberg, Emily S. Barrett, Susan F. Lipson, and Peter T. Ellison. 2002. "Marriage and Fatherhood Are Associated with Lower Testosterone in Males." *Evolution and Human Behavior* 23 (3): 193–201.

Hoffman, Bruce. 2001. "All You Need Is Love: How the Terrorists Stopped Terrorism." *Atlantic Monthly,* December, 17.

Hudson, Valerie M., and Andrea M. den Boer. 2002. "A Surplus of Men, a Deficit of Peace: Security and Sex Ratios in Asia's Largest States." *International Security* 26 (4): 5–38.

——. 2004. *Bare Branches: The Security Implications of Asia's Surplus Male Population.* Cambridge, MA: MIT Press.

Huntington, Samuel P. 1997. *The Clash of Civilizations and the Remaking of World Order.* New York: Touchstone.

Kanazawa, S. (2001). "Why Father Absence Might Precipitate Early Menarche: The Role of Polygyny." *Evolution and Human Behavior* 22(5): 329–34.

Kandiyoti, Deniz. 1994. "The Paradoxes of Masculinity: Some Thoughts on Segregated Societies." In *Dislocating Masculinity: Comparative Ethnographies,* edited by Andrea Cornwall and Nancy Lindisfarne, 197–213. New York: Routledge.

Kepel, Gilles. 2002. *Jihad: The Trail of Political Islam.* Cambridge, MA: Harvard University Press.

Lesthaeghe, Ron, Georgia Kaufmann, Dominique Meekers, and Johan Surkyn. 1994. "Post-Partum Abstinence, Polygyny, and Age at Marriage: A Macro-Level Analysis of Sub-Saharan Societies." In *Nuptiality in Sub-Saharan Africa: Contemporary Anthropological and Demographic Perspectives,* edited by Caroline Bledsoe and Gilles Pison, 25–54. Oxford: Clarendon Press.

Lewis, Bernard. 1993. *Islam and the West.* Oxford: Oxford University Press.

——. 1995. *The Middle East: 2,000 Years of History from the Rise of Christianity to the Present Day.* London: Weidenfeld & Nicolson.

Mazur, Allan, and Alan Booth. 1998. "Testosterone and Dominance in Men." *Behavioral and Brain Sciences* 21:353–63.

Mazur, Allan, and Joel Michalek. 1998. "Marriage, Divorce and Male Testosterone." *Social Forces* 77:315–30.

Mealey, Linda. 2000. *Sex Differences: Developmental and Evolutionary Strategies.* San Diego: Academic Press.

Mernissi, Fatima. 1987. *The Veil and the Male élite: A Feminist Interpretation of Women's Rights in Islam.* Reading, MA: Addison-Wesley.

Mullen, Brian, and Li-Tze Hu. 1989. "Perceptions of Ingroup and Outgroup Variability: A Meta-Analytic Integration." *Basic and Applied Social Psychology* 10:233–52.

Rashid, Ahmed. 2000. *Taliban: Militant Islam, Oil, and Fundamentalism in Central Asia*. New Haven, CT: Yale University Press.

Rosen, Lawrence. 1978. "The Negotiation of Reality: Male-Female Relations in Sefrou, Morocco." In *Women in the Muslim World*, edited by Lois Beck and Nikki R. Keddie, 561–84. Cambridge, MA: Harvard University Press.

Tertilt, Michèle. 2005. "Polygyny, Fertility, and Savings." *Journal of Political Economy* 113 (6): 1341–71

Toubia, Nahid (1994). "Female Circumcision as a Public Health Issue." *New England Journal of Medicine* 331(11): 712–16.

Weisfeld, Glenn E. 1993. "Social Status and Values in Traditional Arab Culture." In *Social Stratification and Socioeconomic Inequality*, vol. 1: *A Comparative Biosocial Analysis*, edited by Lee Ellis, 75–97. Westport, CT: Praeger.

WomanStats Project, http://www.womanstats.org.

4

Attitudes toward Polygyny

Experimental Evidence from Six Countries

Rose McDermott, Michael Dickerson, Steve Fish, Danielle Lussier, and Jonathan Cowden

Polygyny remains a common practice worldwide and has been linked to negative outcomes for women and children. Attitudes regarding additional wives offer a microcosm into decision-making authority within the family, and thus also echo larger societal values reflecting the prevalence of patriarchal structures. It is also important to note the negative effects of polygyny on the majority of poor and low-status men, whose prospects for reproductive access under such a system remain lower. Using an experimental manipulation embedded in six nationally representative samples involving Lebanon, Jordan, Uganda, Indonesia, Mongolia, and two provinces in India (Bihar and the Punjab), we test this simple but essential hypothesis: Does the way that polygyny is framed affect support for it? Specifically, we manipulate whether or not the first wife agrees in asking respondents if a man should take a second wife if he wishes. In addition, regardless of how polygyny is framed, we investigate whether women support polygyny less than men and whether the expressed opinions of men and women about polygyny differ conditioned on question wording. What we find in this sample of over 9,200 respondents is that the first wife's opinion matters in most cases, as too does the demographic profile of respondents, in determining their support for polygyny. But, more important, regardless of frame, respondents generally reject polygyny. We conclude with a discussion of the implications of these findings for states in which polygyny persists.

Typical explanations for threats to national security or economic development center on causes such as violence, including wars, and corrupt or inadequate governance. Yet one of the most parsimonious reasons for poor state outcomes, low rates of economic development, and horrific human security revolve around the prevalence of polygyny and the negative consequences that flow from it (McDermott 2010). For these reasons it is unfortunate that polygyny has been vastly under-studied by scholars of international relations. This is likely, at least in part, because scholars of international relations tend not to recognize marriage as a fundamentally political institution; in fact, marriage is the single most universal of political institutions, existing as the bedrock of family structure, and thus the foundation of national political unity, in essentially every country in the world. While the explanations offered in the literature on state outcomes are no doubt crucial, the prevalence of polygyny influences all aspects of a country's identity, exerting social, economic, and political effects.

Why does polygyny matter so? We discuss the reasons in greater detail below, but, in short, we argue that polygyny constitutes a defining feature of a state because while naturally it represents a form of repression by sex in which men subjugate women, it is also an inherently political institution that seeks to enforce conformity on the population regardless of gender to disproportionately serve and preserve the interests of wealthy and powerful men. While it is true that certain women derive status and economic benefit from its practice, the role of men remains primary. Wealthy and powerful men as a group derive status from the practice of polygyny in the aggregate because they are the predominant beneficiaries of it; however, most men derive no advantage from it and indeed suffer greatly as a result of it, having fewer opportunities to marry themselves. Under this system where wealthier men obtain more than one wife, poorer men, or those with less status or prospects, become marginalized as well. In this sense polygyny as a structure works in the same way as does racism, because its narrative is one of a privileged group, while all the power and reward redound generally only to a small number of them.

Yet if polygyny benefits only the powerful few men at the top of the social ladder and generates problems for everyone else, how does the practice perpetuate itself without the compliance of many of its participants? Who is driving its maintenance? Little systematic exploration and investigation has been brought to bear on this question of support for an institution that causes so many problems for so many. It is time to rectify this oversight and begin to turn the tools of social science to a more systematic exploration of these phenomena. Because some of the literature in economics argues that women themselves often choose polygyny for economic reasons (Becker 1974), and because male desire for sexual variety drives evolutionary explanations for the origin of this kind of marital structure (Kanazawa and Still 2001), the degree to which men and women differ in their support for this institution becomes a critical issue in its maintenance. Experimental methods provide an excellent way to examine differences in these attitudes. Here we report on a massive experiment, involving over nine thousand subjects in six countries, designed to explore these issues.

We begin with a discussion of the negative state and economic outcomes that have been linked to polygyny. We then explain how male and female attitudes matter in determining the nature of marital institutions and describe the experiment we undertake to explore the nature of these attitudes. Finally, we discuss why these findings are significant for macro phenomena such as conflict and economic development.

Polygyny's Negative Outcomes

Polygamy refers to a mating system where individuals have more than one marital partner. It encompasses both polyandry, where one woman has more than one husband, and polygyny, where one man has more than one wife. The former is extremely rare and largely restricted to parts of Nepal and Tibet. But the latter is quite common and occurs in over 70 percent of societies worldwide (Coult and Habenstein 1965).

Polygyny has been systematically linked to a number of important and problematic state outcomes, including levels of economic development and human security. Previous work (McDermott 2010) using data from the WomanStats database including over 170 countries demonstrated that polygyny was significantly associated with such sequelae as high birth rate, high maternal mortality, and low female life expectancy, as well as with high rates of domestic violence, sex trafficking, and female genital mutilation.

Polygyny is also correlated with low conformity with the United Nations Convention on the Elimination of all Forms of Discrimination Against Women and unequal treatment before the law. In additional areas of concern for overall state outcomes, increasing rates of polygyny are associated with higher levels of defense spending, as well as lower levels of civil rights and political liberties around the world (McDermott 2010). Moreover, the concentration of benefits redounds almost exclusively to the men with the most economic, political, and social power; the beneficiaries are small in number. The majority of poorer men have reduced reproductive access because so many women are monopolized by very few men. This is not to say that men and women are equally harmed by polygyny, since women constitute its primary victims, but rather that the majority of both men and women see little to no benefit from the practice and, in fact, are harmed by it, both from an evolutionary standpoint and from within the death grip of class.

In addition, polygyny has been show to retard levels of economic development. In her seminal work on the topic, Michèle Tertilt writes with regard to sub-Saharan Africa that "banning polygyny decreases fertility by 40 percent, increases savings by 70 percent, and increases output per capita by 170 percent" (2005, 1341). In addition, as in our work, she finds that higher rates of polygyny also predict higher spousal age gaps as well.

In addition to the harms that devolve to state outcomes in areas with high rates of sanctioned polygyny, individual injuries derive to many of its most innocent victims, especially the children of such unions. A number of these difficulties have been documented in various studies, particularly in Africa where the practice is most common. Most important, in a study of twenty-two countries in sub-Saharan Africa, children born in polygynous families were much more likely to die than children born into monogamous families (Omariba and Boyle 2007). In addition, children in polygynous families in Tanzania show poorer growth, controlling for other factors (Sellen 1999; Hadley 2005). In Nigeria, polygyny predicts both higher rates of domestic violence (Babalola et al. 2014) as well as much lower household income levels (Lawson 2014). Polygyny imposes costs for both female and male children in other areas as well. It is associated with lower rates of both primary and secondary education.

But such negative outcomes are not restricted to Africa, or to children. For example, Arab Bedouin women in polygynous marriages show significantly higher rates of mental illness, especially depression, than women in monogamous marriages (Daoud et al. 2014). In addition, Morris and Kretzschmar (1997) document concurrent relationships as constituting as important a factor in the spread of HIV as multiple partners. This risk has been most recently demonstrated among Nigerian men (Mitsunaga et al. 2005), although the obvious public health risk of this implication ranges far beyond Africa or even polygynous marital structures.

A polygynous mating system is deleterious for the fitness of males as well. It generates a high proportion of unmated men and is associated with relatively intense male/male competition, including greater rates of violent crime and political conflict, the commitment of more resources to weaponry, and elevated male mortality. Under polygyny the proportion of unmarried men is high, a condition known to be associated with diverse forms of violence and with male social and sexual frustration. Indeed, one of the reasons given for why some states such as Gambia and Togo have outlawed polygyny relates to the desire to equalize reproductive opportunities (Schoellman and Tertilt 2006; Alexander 1974).

The Importance and Relevance of Polygyny for International Relations

Obviously, polygyny would not pose an issue for international relations if it were a rare phenomenon. However, its prevalence both historically and in modern societies, while often geographically concentrated, nevertheless appears endemic. In the Human Relations Area Files Ethnographic Atlas of over 1,200 societies, kept since 1949, polygyny occurs in over a thousand of them. However, many governments and international bodies are beginning to recognize the harms that result from such marital institutions and are seeking to ban them. For example, polygyny is considered to violate the International Covenant on Political and Civil Rights, and the United Nations has called for its abolition. In the recent court case in Canada which was discussed in chapter 3, polygyny was found to constitute a violation to international human rights law, and a ban on its practice was upheld.

Nevertheless, in spite of increasingly widespread governmental recognition of the harms that derive from polygynous practices, and the many empirical studies that support these conclusions, scholars of international relations and other political scientists have tended to neglect, if not outright ignore, its relevance for achieving international and state security. Doubtless one of the reasons for this lies in the implicit belief that personal marital practices and structures constitute microlevel phenomena with limited or no relevance to macrolevel outcomes of primary interest to such scholars.

Yet the evidence described above pokes clear holes in such beliefs because polygyny is not simply a matter of who marries whom; it is instead a policed and framed way of managing resource allocation between groups and also within groups. Strange though it may seem in certain societies, polygyny easily slips into the realm of politics in terms of who gets what, when, and how. In other words, different patterns of marriage allocate resources to men, women, and children in different ways. Put another way, societies with polygyny are organized in fundamental and multiple ways that are different from those that do not support the practice. To be sure, different does not necessarily mean worse, but the fact of its existence demands an investigation of its causes and consequences.

As a result, it behooves those interested in exploring the documented relationship between the security of women and its relationship to the security of states (Hudson et al. 2008/9) to undertake additional empirical exploration of the attitudes, behaviors, and institutions that undergird and sustain polygynous practices. Specifically, it is important to provide a better and more systematic understanding of the relationship between microlevel practices in powerful and ubiquitous family institutions such as marriage with macrolevel outcomes such as conflict and development.

Since the seminal work of Gary Becker (1974) on the economics of marriage, many economists have examined the role of economic incentives in determining the structure of marriage and have sought to characterize male–female relationships in terms of marriage markets, discussing incentives, rewards, and costs as in any other market relationship. Subsequent work by Grossbard (1978) attempted to integrate the insights of anthropology with economics to create a more comprehensive and socially sensitive model of the role of marriage in society. In a controversial argument, Kanazawa and Still (2001) argued for a female choice theory of marriage, suggesting that polygyny could be driven, at least in part, by women who prefer more resources as an additional wife of a wealthier man over fewer resources that might result from monogamous marriage to a poorer one. Sanderson (2001) for one disputes this argument, supporting Alexander's idea that states should encourage monogamy to equalize reproductive access for men. He argues that the empirical data support the notion of male, as opposed to female, choice driving marriage decisions.

Comparing these perspectives, polygyny can be seen to present both economic and social rewards and incentives that confer differentially to men, helping to perpetuate patterns of patriarchy that remain detrimental not only to women and children but to many lower-status and lower-income men as well. In many evolutionary arguments, such patterns of patriarchy are seen to emerge, at least in part, from enhanced male/male competition for reproductive access and control (Divale and Harris 1976; Ember, Ember, and Low 2007; Mitani, Gros-Louis, and Richards 1996; Smuts 1992, 1995). For this reason, among others, several states including Gambia, Togo, and Canada have sought to render polygyny illegal.

Such attempts to ban polygyny have proven difficult, however, encountering not just cultural opposition but real economic challenges to prosperous men in particular during the transitional phase from polygyny to monogamy (Schoellman and Tertilt 2006), making change difficult to implement. Moreover, scholars such as Anderson (2000) argue that polygyny emerges in response to poverty, while scholars such as Barber (2008) argue that resource defense, sex ratio, and pathogen avoidance similarly encourage polygynous practices in places with high inequality in the distribution of wealth or high rates of infectious disease; importantly, he finds no evidence for religious or gender discrimination in perpetuating polygynous practices, claiming such culturally determinist accounts lack empirical validity.

The Role of Attitudes in Sustaining Polygynous Practices

One of the factors maintaining the practice of polygyny is obviously the attitudes and behaviors of those who choose to participate in, or reject, such marital unions. Yet these attitudes have not been studied in a rigorous way. Indeed, one of the fundamental issues in polygynous societies revolves around the extent to which men and women in such cultures sanction polygyny or view female objections to it as important in constraining male choice. Given the harms that follow from the widespread practice of polygyny, it is important to understand these attitudes and the micropractices that might sustain these patterns of behavior that help perpetuate patriarchy in ways that prove harmful to men, women, children, and society as a whole as described above.

Experimental methods provide the means to examine these very factors, allowing representative samples and controlled manipulation in order to begin to tackle how microlevel decision-making processes affect macrolevel institutional outcomes. We employ an experimental treatment that enables us to gain insight into how a first wife's opinion on her husband's taking a second wife affects respondents' views on the acceptability of polygynous marriage. We never ask the respondent to put him/herself in the position of making a decision about their own behavior. Rather, we present the scenario to respondents and ask whether or not a third party should take a wife under two controlled conditions, one where the first wife does not object to her husband taking a second wife, and the second where she does. In this way, we are essentially measuring social tolerance or acceptance of polygyny by measuring endorsement or rejection of a social norm; this construction also allows us to look at society's evaluation of whether the first wife's opinion should matter in the husband's decision making about a practice that affects them both. In so doing, we hope to shed light on how the balance of power in the household between men and women might serve either to perpetuate or diminish macro practices that sustain patriarchy within the aggregate macro institutions of society. To achieve a degree of generalizability, we undertake this study in six countries that vary in their level of development, as well as other cultural and societal factors such as dominant religion, to gain traction on the sources of similarity as well as gain insight into some of the potential foundations of variance in attitudes across countries. Further, our experimental design allows us to examine whether and how men and women might differ in their opinions toward this practice, as well as to explore the influence of various demographic factors, such as education and income, on respondents' attitudes toward polygyny.

In general, our argument is that the determinants of polygyny revolve around the way the practice is framed, the demographic "identity" of the person who is asked to evaluate it, and possible ways in which the identity of a person and the way the question is framed interact. An example of framing might be that men and women both support polygyny in some cases more than others, as for instance if a first wife approves of or opposes her husband's marrying a second wife. An example of how identity might influence response could occur if women as a group showed greater opposition to polygyny than men as a group. An example of the interaction of framing and identity might be that when polygyny is difficult to oppose, men and women do so in the same way, whereas when polygyny is more difficult to support, men do so more frequently than do women because fundamentally power relations in these societies have a gendered component to them. We hypothesize that women, in general, will be less accepting of additional wives than men regardless of frame because the benefits of sequential spouses accrue almost entirely to men; the division of resources, including time and attention, between wives can serve only to potentially harm women and their children in all the ways documented above.

Methods

To investigate this and other questions, we undertook a survey experiment embedded in nationally representative samples in six countries: Jordan, Lebanon, Uganda, Indonesia, Mongolia, and two provinces in India (Bihar and the Punjab). This question constituted part of a larger study focused on attitudes toward gender equality. We chose countries that differed in their geography, as well as their level of economic development, because these variables might account for any differences we uncover. In addition, because one of our variables of interest related to how the religion of respondents might affect their attitudes, we chose countries that differed in their dominant religious affiliation because we expected many of the attitudes toward sexual equality we interrogate might be related to the confessional adherence of participants.

The first experimental item assesses the question we interrogate here, which focuses on the acceptability of polygynous marriage. Specifically, we ask whether a first wife's objection to her husband's desire to take a second wife should influence his decision on whether to take a second wife. (Although we could have, we did not ask about the potential opinion of the second wife, assuming she would not marry if she were able to voice objection.

The exact same question was presented to each respondent with only one aspect of the question manipulated. In the question we grapple with, only the first wife's preference was manipulated between versions. The specific question we examine is presented as follows. The name of the man in the question is drawn from the survey of Indonesia.

A) Pak Mahmud is married and currently has one wife. According to his religious tradition, it is acceptable to have more than one wife. He is financially secure and able to provide for a second wife. He would like to marry a second woman, but his first wife objects. Should Pak Mahmud take a second wife?
   a) Yes
   b) No
   OR
B) Pak Mahmud is married and currently has one wife. According to his religious tradition, it is acceptable to have more than one wife. He is financially secure and able to provide for a second wife. He would like to marry a second woman, and his first wife has not objected. Should Pak Mahmud take a second wife?
   a) Yes
   b) No

Each question represents an independent manipulation, meaning that one version of each question was randomly administered to half of the sample, and its other version to the other half. Responses to the alternative versions can be compared because they frame the exact same subject matter in different ways, such as described above regarding polygyny. Not only are the questions randomly assigned, but the samples of population to which the questions are administered are also randomly drawn. This in turn means that respondents should mirror national demographics such as sex, religion, age, education, income, and rural versus urban residences. In each country, we administered the survey to approximately 1,200 people, although that number was higher (2,958) in India; exact numbers differed slightly by country and question, and the specific sample sizes are depicted in the tables and figures presented in the results section. Results are reported separately for each country below.

Results

Considering support for polygyny collapsed across question versions but considering each country differently, it can be concluded that the practice is generally unpopular. If these countries were operating in all phases conditional on a simple rule of democratic functioning within the government, one could expect this practice would be on unstable ground if its support did not hover at more than 50 percent. Of course, the polity need not reflect the underlying level of popular opinion, but as a heuristic tool it is useful to know the level of support for this practice in the population. So it is with popular level of support that we will make judgments about polygyny's level of support.

The substantive hypothesis that support for polygyny is 50 percent or less can be tested statistically with a difference of proportions test. What we would like to know is whether level of support for polygyny is less than 50 percent. This we formulate as the alternative hypothesis versus the null hypothesis that this support is 50 percent or greater. In all but one case, the statistical tests reveal that we reject the null hypothesis at any standard cut point. That exception is Uganda, where support for polygyny is much greater than it is elsewhere. In this country, the hypothesis that support is 50 percent or greater cannot be rejected.

But this perhaps is not the best way of evaluating the absolute level of support for this practice. Depending on the frame, the level of support will change, and as a result, a more difficult test of whether there is majority support would turn on a framing of it as justifiable. Or put differently, what happens when we choose the question version most likely to generate support among a demographic group that derives at least the benefits of status from the practice? That would be the level of support for version B among men, or that group's response to the frame "when the first wife does not object." The idea is that this version provides them with a reason for supporting the practice. After all, if a wife does not object and polygyny is seen by men as justified even in certain instances, their response to that practice is informed by the knowledge that the wife does not object.

In essence, the question legitimates the practice by indicating that a stakeholder does not oppose it. But even with this practice seemingly without opposition from the family, the fact remains that the practice is not popular in the countries we examine, save in Uganda. In short, the practice is not supported in large numbers.

Let us now move to examine the empirical support for our hypotheses about the effects of question wording in a model in which support for polygyny is proposed to be a function of question wording, the sex of the respondent, and an interaction between these latter two variables. Because polygyny is a binary variable, we use logistic regression as our means of testing our hypotheses. We predict an effect for question wording based on whether the first wife approves or disapproves of her husband taking a second wife, as described above. Specifically, we anticipate that the odds of supporting polygyny increase when the wife does not object, controlling for other variables in the model. Methodologically, because version B is the more restrictive frame and version A is the baseline, the odds ratio will be less than one, controlling for other covariates in the model. So our statistical test compares the null hypothesis, which is that the coefficient is one or more, with the alternative, which is that the odds ratio is less than one.

Not only do we anticipate an effect of the wording independent of any other covariates in the model, we also anticipate an effect for gender. The dummy variable that is used for gender in the logistic regression has women as its reference category. So what we expect to find unless there are interaction terms that are significant is support among men for polygyny that is larger than support among women regardless of question version. Thus formulated, the null hypothesis for this variable is that the odds ratio should be higher than one, and the alternative one that the odds ratio should be one or less. While the expectations above assume that the question wording's effect operates the same even if conditioned on gender, this need not be so. Enter here the possibility of heterogeneous treatment effects. This literature argues that randomizing the treatment/control is not enough because the effect of this randomization may be conditioned on the group that is administering the test. It seems plausible that sex may condition the effect of question wording. In the simplest terms, the substantive point is that men and women may prefer to inhabit different worlds because what the experiment manipulates is the meaning of polygyny as a social, economic, and political phenomenon. Viewed with greater nuance, what these meanings encompass may differ in each of the polities we examine. Gender roles can be expressed as permissible and sanctioned means of expression and identity, both within and across countries. The point is not that in each society a particular set of sanctioned roles determines how men and women behave in lockstep, only that expressed preferences cannot be unshackled from the expectations of society and the specific desires of different groups that inhabit it.

The question is how these expressed preferences manifest differently within different groups or layers of society. The likeliest possibility is not easy to pinpoint because it asks for a good answer to the question of whether men or women see "differences of differences" in what those wordings entail. If social structures argue in favor of polygyny, then women would need a compelling reason to publically report an opinion against it and, indeed, to identify one if a potentially reasonable possibility were offered to them. Under this scenario it seems unlikely that men would contextualize polygyny as a nuanced rather than an all-or-nothing possibility. Believing it just and reasonable, men would then view a prompt noting how the wife of a husband feels as irrelevant: knowing that a husband wishes a particular outcome is all the information required for them. Or it might be that women oppose polygyny at very high levels, but men may not feel as strongly, leaving open the possibility that men can more easily move away from a baseline of support because that provides them with more flexibility in their opinions. Note that such flexibility does not in itself mean that men are "gender neutral" in their beliefs, only that they can become more so if provided with the right context to express that position. Certainly, these do not exhaust the universe of reasonable but conflicting hypotheticals about the nature of the interaction term, and because of that we find no compelling reason to preference any one of them over the others. Our view is that the results should speak for themselves, which statistically means two-tailed tests for all of the reported coefficients in the models. In other words, our null hypothesis about the interaction term is that it should be statistically indistinguishable from one, whereas the alternative hypothesis is that the interaction term is different from one at conventional levels of statistical significance.

In considering our hypotheses, we will begin with a brief discussion of the odds ratios as ways of conceptualizing the relationships in the data when there are only main effects. We will spend some time with the meaning of an interaction term, since the presence of such moderates the effects of the variables and exhibits a heterogeneous treatment effect. This is because the odds for, say, the effect of question wording depend on whether the respondent is male or female. Following that, we will look at probabilities.

The average marginal effects are reported separately from the odds ratios, as too are the plots of estimated probabilities. These will reveal how the probability of support for polygyny is contingent on the variables in the model, including the sex of the respondent. Because changes in the plotted slopes are visual representations of the effects of question version conditioned on the sex of the respondent, we can chart the effects of the two variables as these operate in tandem by using graphs of marginal effects. We are particularly interested in whether the slopes for the two lines run parallel to one other, since when these are not parallel, the effects of wording are conditioned by the sex of the respondent: men and women change (slope of the line) in different ways in response to the treatment. This would be another way of saying that there are differences in how the same changes in wording are processed and reported by men and women in different ways. So there is no one meaning of polygyny, but somewhat contested ones depending on the sex of the respondent. What polygyny means depends on who must interpret it.

Let us now turn to the results. We present the findings for, respectively, Jordan, Lebanon, Uganda, Indonesia, India, and Mongolia. The statistical significance of a coefficient is not mentioned further unless it does not meet the conventional significant level of 0.05. The results for Jordan are presented in Table 4.1. Here both of our expectations are supported, as can be seen from the odds ratios, the average marginal effects, and the graph expressing the probability of support for polygyny. The odds ratio for the question wording variables shows that those in version A of the wording are 0.22 as likely as those in version B to support polygyny; recall again that this distinction reflects the effect of whether or not the first wife

TABLE 4.1. The Effects of Wording and Gender in Jordan, Lebanon, and Uganda

VARIABLES	Jordan	Lebanon	Uganda
Version A or Version B	0.215**	0.400**	0.772
	(0.062)	(0.097)	(0.125)
Gender	2.071**	1.948**	1.231
	(0.380)	(0.367)	(0.199)
Interaction	1.227	1.604	0.944
	(0.430)	(0.485)	(0.216)
Observations	1,200	1,200	1,235
χ^2 test, 3 df	88.075	49.631	8.604
p-value	0.000	0.000	0.035

** $p<0.01$, * $p<0.05$, + $p<0.1$

Notes: The reported coefficients are odds ratios. The associated robust standard errors are reported in parentheses. A decision rule of $\alpha < 0.05$ is used to evaluate the fit of the coefficients and overall model.

TABLE 4.2. Average Marginal Effects for All Six Countries

Country	Gender	Question Wording		Significance of Difference	
		Version A	*Version B*	*Difference*	*p*-value
Jordan	*Female*	0.059	0.226	−0.167	0.000
	Male	0.138	0.376	−0.239	0.000
Lebanon	*Female*	0.096	0.210	−0.114	0.000
	Male	0.249	0.341	−0.092	0.012
Uganda	*Female*	0.436	0.500	−0.064	0.107
	Male	0.473	0.522	−0.049	0.050
Indonesia	*Female*	0.123	0.371	−0.248	0.000
	Male	0.213	0.500	−0.287	0.000
India	*Female*	0.260	0.284	−0.025	0.314
	Male	0.269	0.357	−0.088	0.000
Mongolia	*Female*	0.164	0.296	−0.132	0.000
	Male	0.194	0.351	−0.157	0.000

(Note this should be relabeled "Table 4.2")

disapproves (A) or approves (B) of the husband taking a second wife. The odds ratio of 2.07 indicates that men are more likely than women to support polygyny, and by quite a margin.

Table 4.2 reports the findings in terms of average marginal effects rather than odds ratios. Considering women first, the difference in the

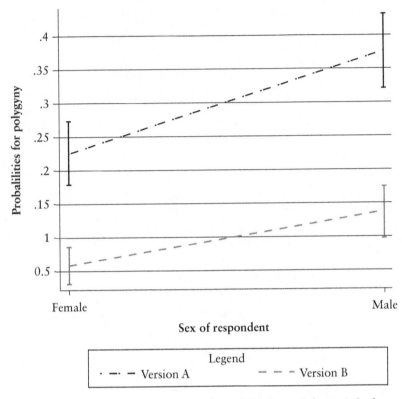

Figure 4.1. The Marginal Effects of Gender and Wording on Polygyny in Jordan
Note: 95% confidence intervals.

probability of supporting polygyny is higher for version B than version A (0.226 versus 0.059). A similar finding obtains for men. Figure 4.1 may be interpreted first as indicating the lack of an interaction between the two variables. Particularly, it maps how these change, if at all, as a function of question wording and gender. The line represented in Figure 4.1 is hypothetical, of course, because we are speaking of discrete rather than continuous changes—men versus women. But what can be known from the slopes of the line is whether the effect of question wording is conditioned by gender. When the slopes differ, there is an interaction. And when there is not an interaction, the substantive meaning is that changes in the question wording have equal effects for both men and women.

The bars around the points are confidence intervals. Whether differences are statistically significant turns on possible overlap in these intervals, or substantively, whether responses of men and women are alike enough statistically to regard them as identical when responding to changes in the question wording. Note here that men and women can respond differently to each of the pairs of wordings. Women could always view polygyny as more aversive than men, regardless of which of the prompts they are given. So for version A, there is a given difference between men and women, as too there is for version B. But the bottom line is that the slopes of the hypothetical line tell us whether the reaction to wording is conditioned on gender, or put differently, whether an interaction between gender and wording exists. The data indicate that in Jordan no such interaction exists. Men and women differ in their response to the question, but the differences themselves do not change based on changes in wording. Women are always more likely than men to oppose polygyny, and the difference in responses is replicated for both versions A and B.

The findings for Lebanon conform to those in Jordan. First, as Table 4.1 attests, support for a second wife turns partly on the question version: those asked version A are 0.40 times as likely as those asked question version B to support polygyny. Women are far less supportive than men of polygyny; in fact, the odds of men supporting polygyny are almost two times more likely than the odds of women doing so. Because there is no interaction term, we may say that these results are not conditioned by sex of respondent. Table 4.2 shows that question wording has an effect for both men and women when considering average marginal effect. The lines in Figure 4.2 are roughly parallel to one another, and the confidence intervals do not cross either for men or for women, demonstrating that men and women respond similarly to the experimental effect.

The third country is Uganda. Scanning Table 4.1, no significant findings appear. Indeed, every odds ratio is not statistically different from zero using a standard measure of statistical significance. Table 4.2 of average marginal effects indicates that there is a statistically significant difference in the probability of version A differenced from version B. Men do become more supportive according to this analysis. Why this is so is not immediately clear. Far from its being the case that women have floor levels of support for polygyny regardless of condition, roughly equal proportions of support for polygyny exist for women in question versions A and

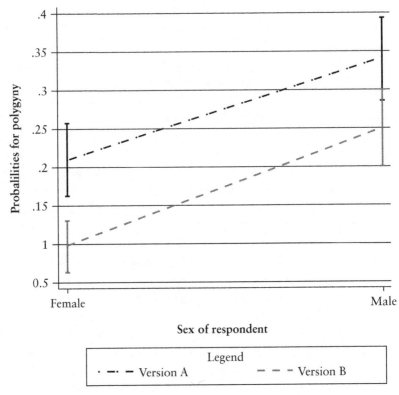

Figure 4.2. The Marginal Effects of Gender and Wording on Polygyny in Lebanon
Note: 95% confidence intervals.

B. Based on the slope of the lines in Figure 4.3, one could conclude that men become more supportive when comparing version B versus version A, whereas women retain an equal level of support. Curiously, the confidence bands do cross. The exact nature of the effect of sex on response to question wording is thus in question.

In Indonesia, effects consistent with our original expectations return. Whether seen from the view of odds ratios (Table 4.3), average marginal effects (Table 4.2), or the plots of probabilities (Figure 4.4), the question version matters. It is also the case that sex of respondent matters, and in the predicted direction. The coefficient for the odds ratio indicates that the odds that men support polygyny are 1.7 times that of women. There is no evidence of an interaction between gender and question wording, or substantively, that men and women are different in the way that they view

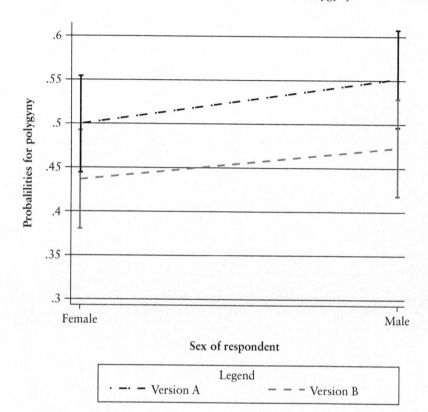

Figure 4.3. The Marginal Effects of Gender and Wording on Polygyny in Uganda
Note: 95% confidence intervals.

TABLE 4.3. The Effects of Wording and Gender in Indonesia, India, and Mongolia

VARIABLES	Indonesia	India	Mongolia
Version A or Version B	0.238**	0.883	0.466**
	(0.051)	(0.109)	(0.080)
Male or Female	1.695**	1.400**	1.286
	(0.289)	(0.158)	(0.201)
Interaction	1.139	0.748+	0.957
	(0.321)	(0.123)	(0.240)
N	1,171	2,925	1,472
χ^2 test, 3 df	107.938	22.136	43.209
p-value	0.000	0.000	0.000

** $p<0.01$, * $p<0.05$, + $p<0.1$

Notes: The reported coefficients are odds ratios. The associated robust standard errors are reported in parentheses. A decision rule of $\alpha < 0.05$ is used to evaluate the fit of the coefficients and overall model.

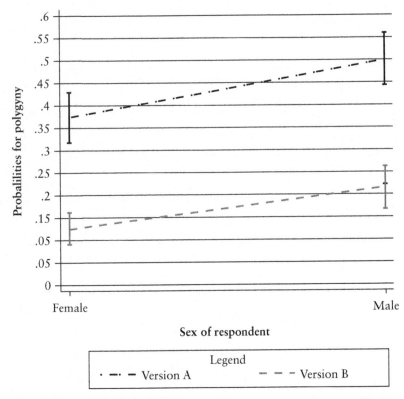

Figure 4.4. The Marginal Effects of Gender and Wording on Polygyny in Indonesia
Note: 95% confidence intervals.

this manipulation. This does not indicate that there are no wording pairs that would prompt men and women to respond differently, but rather that this version does not.

India is another story. As can be seen in Table 4.3, question wording does not appear to have an effect, but the sex of the respondent does, as also does the interaction between sex and question wording. So we can't say that question wording has a single effect, or that the sex of the respondent does, either. Turning to the results as evidenced by probabilities, as presented in Table 4.2, these data show that women are not affected by the change in the question version, whereas men are. Again, this is something of a puzzle because women are not absolutely opposed to polygyny and therefore immune to the change in wording. As was the case earlier,

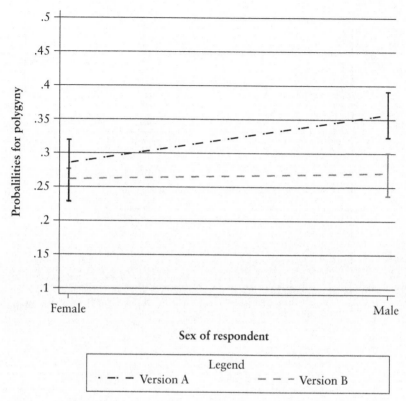

Figure 4.5. The Marginal Effects of Gender and Wording on Polygyny in India
Note: 95% confidence intervals.

the results indicate that for men it does matter whether they receive the treatment or the control condition. Figure 4.5 brings home what is occurring in visual form. Manipulating the version of the question appears not to affect women at all; there is nearly no slope whatsoever. But for men, there is a definite effect because of the upward slope of the line and the final difference in effects.

We conclude with Mongolia. Statistical analysis shows that there is an effect for question wording. Starting with Table 4.3, note that the odds ratio is statistically significant and shows that respondents in version A are 0.47 times as likely as those in version B to support polygyny. There is no effect for gender and no support for the hypothesis of a nonzero interaction tern. As shown in Table 4.2, male and female respondents react

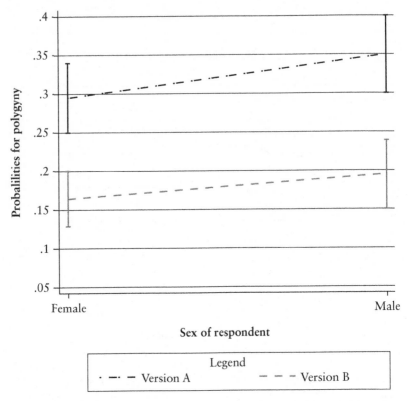

Figure 4.6. The Marginal Effects of Gender and Wording on Polygyny in Mongolia
Note: 95% confidence intervals.

roughly equally to the manipulation. Figure 4.6 brings home the point by demonstrating an effect for question wording regardless of gender.

Discussion and Conclusion

It stands to reason that were the choices of the majority of individuals obeyed, and with the benefits deriving to men themselves very selective in nature, some mechanism is required to police, enforce, and perpetuate the practice of polygyny. Policing of course includes violence, and a good bit of evidence suggests that a state will employ it to perpetuate the subjugation of marginalized group members, including women. But states have an easier time policing a population they can persuade rather than coerce into compliance. So public opinion also remains an important tool in sustaining any kind of political institution that requires some degree of adherence to continue. We examine just such public opinion toward polygyny among over nine thousand men and women across six countries, manipulating the degree to which a woman opposes her husband taking another wife.

But we have additional findings as well. There are some interesting similarities and some equally provocative differences in our examination of individuals' responses to the question of whether a husband should take a second wife contingent on whether or not the first wife objects. In most cases, as we expected, we find a main effect of question wording on responses, such that most individuals are more accepting of polygyny when the first wife does not object to the husband's taking a second wife. The notable exception in this case is Uganda, although results here may simply reflect the reality that polygyny is a much more common occurrence there than in our other cases. For example, in the WomanStats database, Uganda is the only country we examine that achieves a maximum value of 4 on a 0–4 scale, where 4 reflects that at least 25 percent of women live in polygynous unions; all the other countries we examine rank at 2 or below, except Jordan, which has a value of 3.

Additionally, as expected, men tend to respond differently to the question of polygyny than do women. In general, they are more supportive than women of polygyny, regardless of whether or not the first wife objects. In Uganda, there are no effects of gender whatsoever: no main effect and no moderating one, either. This may appear strange given the treatment, but it is nonetheless understandable. Uganda appears to have a strong historical tradition supporting polygyny, which permeates its contemporary society. Consequently, polygyny holds a "memory" or what could arguably be called structures that exhibit what economists refer to as an autoregressive process. Autoregressive processes govern change because they limit its scope. Depending on how strong the effect of the baseline is, potential causes of change will produce incremental shifts rather than dramatic ones.

Consider a perceptual equivalent to that: if the wording constitutes a proposed change to the social order, autoregressive processes could be said to occur if responses to that change are very small. Entrenched social processes dictate what people believe and therefore what they will say. In essence and framed statistically, while the constant term for other countries constitutes a baseline effect, such that other odds ratios represent changes from it, in Uganda that odds ratio becomes mathematically and substantively the best guess we have of the absolute level of support there is for polygyny. This finding may reflect the greater cultural acceptance of polygyny in Uganda. However, in this examination, Mongolia also fails to demonstrate the expected sex differences in response, and they do not have the same historical endorsement of the practice. As a result, further research across a broader range of countries may prove necessary to disentangle the effects of history and culture from the more proximal effects exerted by decision-making authority in the household over important family matters. These differences raise interesting possibilities for the investigation of the basis of sex differences in attitudes to various practices that affect gender equality, in this case in the domain of polygyny.

A couple of interesting points of conclusion are worth raising. First, it is both affirming and intriguing that we have found significant differences in attitudes toward polygyny based on both question wording and the sex of respondent in the majority of the samples we have collected. These findings provide encouraging evidence that significant differences on important dimensions of everyday human experience can be illuminated by a methodological mechanism such as ours. Substantively, the variances in attitudes we report suggest that polygyny continues to represent an important mechanism by which gender inequality is perpetuated; women may have an effect on men's behavior in this domain, but this effect is not always decisive and differs by culture and country in intensity and significance. Second, these findings show that conducting the exact same experiment embedded in a nationally representative sample across many countries allows investigators to traction additional analytic leverage by helping locate the sources of potential similarities as well as differences across different national contexts as well as population subgroups found in all national contexts.

Finally, while a theory of biological markets may help explain why wealthier men have greater access to women in a polygynous system such as Uganda, it cannot adequately explain the costs of such a system on women (Pollet and Nettle 2009). While such costs are associated to varying extents with gross domestic product (GDP) and sex ratio, the fact that the correlations remain independent of GDP and sex ratio demands explanation. Attitudes toward such practices offer one such vector by which patriarchal practices get replicated and even reified in various institutional forms, including decision making between man and wife at the household level. We have shown that women may oppose such practices, but their opinions may not matter if they are overridden by their husbands and other male relatives. Intensified male coercion is a likely explanation for women in more polygynous countries experiencing more negative outcomes when their voice is not heard in the family, marketplace, or political arena. The fact that discrepancy and gender inequity were also associated with greater polygyny strongly supports the male coercion hypothesis. Polygynous marriage systems in contemporary countries thus appear to conform to the expectations of sexual selection theory through their association with coercive costs differentially experienced by women.

References

Alexander, Richard D. 1974. "The Evolution of Social Behavior." *Annual Review of Ecology and Systematics* 5:325–83.

Anderson, Connie M. 2000. "The Persistence of Polygyny as an Adaptive Response to Poverty and Oppression in Apartheid South Africa." *Cross-Cultural Research* 34:99–112.

Babalola, D. A., P. E. Omeonu, C. O. Agbede, T. A. Odewusi, and M. F. Olanrewaju. 2014. "Assessing the Economic Burden and Determinants of Violence among Households in Ogun State, Nigeria." *IOSR Journal of Humanities and Social Science* 19 (9): 62–68.

Barber, Nigel. 2008. "Explaining Cross-National Differences in Polygyny Intensity: Resource-Defense, Sex Ratio, and Infectious Diseases. *Cross-Cultural Research* 42:103–17.

Becker, G. S. 1974. "A Theory of Marriage." In *Economics of the Family: Marriage, Children, and Human Capital*, edited by Theodore W. Schultz, 299–351. Chicago: University of Chicago Press.

Coult, Allan D., and Robert W. Habenstein. 1965. *Cross Tabulations of Murdock's World Ethnographic Sample*. Columbia: University of Missouri Press.

Daoud, Nihaya, Ilana Shoham-Vardi, Marcelo Louis Urquia, and Patricia O'Campo. 2014. "Polygamy and Poor Mental Health among Arab Bedouin Women: Do Socioeconomic Position and Social Support Matter?" *Ethnicity & Health* 19 (4): 385–405.

Divale, William Tulio, and Marvin Harris. 1976. "Population, Warfare and the Male Supremacist Complex." *American Anthropologist* 78:521–38.

Ember, Melvin, Carol R. Ember, and Bobbi S. Low. 2007. "Comparing Explanations of Polygyny." *Cross-Cultural Research* 41:428–40.

Grossbard, Amyra. 1978. "Towards a Marriage between Economics and Anthropology and a General Theory of Marriage." *American Economic Review* 68 (2): 33–37.

Hadley, Craig. 2005. "Is Polygyny a Risk Factor for Poor Growth Performance among Tanzanian Agropastoralists?" *American Journal of Physical Anthropology* 126 (4): 471–80.

Hudson, Valerie M., Mary Caprioli, Bonnie Ballif-Spanvill, Rose McDermott, and Chad F. Emmett. 2008/9. "The Heart of the Matter: The Security of Women and the Security of States." *International Security* 33 (3): 7–45.

Kanazawa, Satoshi, and Mary C. Still. 2001. "The Emergence of Marriage Norms: An Evolutionary Psychological Perspective." In *Social Norms*, edited by Michael Hechter and Karl-Dieter Opp, 274–304. New York: Russell Sage Foundation.

Lawson, Ponnie Solomon. 2014. "The World Bank Poverty Line and Marital Forms in Nigeria's South Western States of Osun and Oyo." *International Journal of Humanities, Social Sciences and Education* 1 (10): 18–24.

McDermott, Rose. 2010. "Expert Report Prepared for the Attorney General of Canada." http://stoppolygamyincanada.files.wordpress.com/2011/04/mcdermott-report.pdf.

Mitani, J. C., J. Gros-Louis, and A. F. Richards. 1996. "Sexual Dimorphism, the Operational Sex Ratio, and the Intensity of Male Competition in Polygynous Primates." *American Naturalist* 147:966–80.

Mitsunaga, Tisha M., Antonia M. Powell, Nathan J. Heard, and Ulla M. Larsen. 2005. "Extramarital Sex among Nigerian Men: Polygyny and Other Risk Factors." *JAIDS: Journal of Acquired Immune Deficiency Syndrome* 39 (4): 478–88.

Morris, Martina, and Mirjam Kretzschmar. 1997. "Concurrent Partnerships and the Spread of HIV." *Aids* 11 (5): 641–48.

Omariba, D. Walter Rasugu, and Michael H. Boyle. 2007. "Family Structure and Child Mortality in Sub-Saharan Africa: Cross-National Effects of Polygyny." *Journal of Marriage and Family* 69 (2): 528–43.

Pollet, Thomas V., and Daniel Nettle. 2009. "Market Forces Affect Patterns of Polygyny in Uganda." *Proceedings of the National Academy of Sciences* 106 (7): 2114–17.

Sanderson, Stephen K. 2001. "Explaining Monogamy and Polygyny in Human Societies: Comment on Kanazawa and Still." *Social Forces* 80:329–35.

Schoellman, Todd, and Michèle Tertilt. 2006. "Marriage Laws and Growth in Sub-Saharan Africa." *American Economic Review* 96 (2): 295–98.

Sellen, Daniel W. 1999. "Polygyny and Child Growth in a Traditional Pastoral Society." *Human Nature* 10:329–71.

Smuts, Barbara. 1992. "Male Aggression against Women: An Evolutionary Perspective." *Human Nature* 3:1–44.

——. 1995. "The Evolutionary Origins of Patriarchy." *Human Nature* 6:1–32.

Tertilt, Michèle. 2005. "Polygyny, Fertility, and Savings." *Journal of Political Economy* 113 (6): 1341–71.

Comment 1

THE CANADIAN POLYGAMY REFERENCE

Demonstrating Harms to the Court

B. J. Wray

On October 22, 2009, the lieutenant governor in council of British Columbia asked the Supreme Court of British Columbia (BCSC) to conduct a hearing into the constitutionality of the Criminal Code of Canada's prohibition on polygamy. The polygamy offense first appeared in the Criminal Code in 1892, and in the years following the enactment of the Canadian Charter of Rights and Freedoms in 1982, questions arose as to the Charter compliance of the prohibition on polygamy. Various levels of government, as well as civil libertarians and some religious organizations, wondered if the prohibition might offend the Charter's guarantees of religious freedom and life, liberty, and security of the person. Given the existence of a large community of Fundamentalist Latter Day Saints (FLDS) in Bountiful, British Columbia, the province had a particular interest in the constitutionality of the polygamy offense and decided, after many years of legal opinions from government lawyers as well as outside counsel, to obtain an opinion from the BCSC.

The chief justice of the BCSC was appointed to hear the reference proceeding. The attorney general of Canada (AGC) along with the attorney general of British Columbia (AGBC) defended the constitutionality of the prohibition, while an amicus curiae was appointed by the chief justice to argue that the prohibition was unconstitutional. In addition to these three primary participants, the chief justice permitted eleven advocacy organizations to intervene in the proceedings. These organizations represented a wide spectrum of ideological and constitutional perspectives that included civil libertarians, polyamorists, feminists, conservative religious groups, and children's advocates. The breadth of the evidence submitted in the proceeding was extraordinary and led the chief justice to remark that his decision was based on "the most comprehensive judicial record on the subject ever produced" (*Reference*, para. 6).

I was one of the lawyers representing the AGC in the proceedings. In Canada, responsibility for determining the content of the Criminal Code falls on the federal government. The provinces, however, have responsibility for prosecuting Criminal Code offenses. In the Polygamy Reference, the AGC and the AGBC worked together to ensure that we did not duplicate our evidence-gathering efforts. From the outset, my colleagues and I determined that the AGC would seek out evidence on the big-picture harms associated with the practice of polygamy around the world, while counsel for the AGBC decided to focus primarily on the on-the-ground harms of polygamy as seen in the FLDS and other polygamist communities in North America.

When I began my research into the effects associated with the practice of polygamy, I quickly realized that the existing literature tended to focus on either discrete effects or particular geographical locations/cultures. I could not locate the type of big-picture analysis that I hoped would assist the chief justice in understanding the inherent or universal harms of polygamy. Without such an analysis, it would be an uphill battle to convince the chief justice that the problems associated with polygamy in a foreign country would apply equally to the practice of polygamy in Canada.

And then I found Professor McDermott's work. A colleague came across a media article citing Professor's McDermott's early statistical analysis of the effects of polygyny.[1] This was precisely the type of analysis

---

1. "Polygamy" is an umbrella terms that refers to having more than one spouse at the same time. It includes "polygyny" (a male having multiples wives) and "polyandry" (a female having multiple husbands). In the Polygamy Reference, nearly all of the witnesses used "polygamy" to mean "polygyny," and I generally do the same in this article. However, I use the terminology that the particular witness used when describing their evidence. Professor McDermott exclusively analyzed "polygyny."

I was looking for, and, to my knowledge, no one else had attempted such a wide-ranging statistical analysis of the potential impacts of polygyny across cultures, across nations, and across geographical locations. The existing literature was certainly useful in understanding specific instances of polygyny, but it could not establish a meaningful statistically significant relationship between polygyny and its effects. I hoped that Professor McDermott's analysis could establish the universality of polygyny's effects and the generalizability of these effects to a wider population. All I needed to do was convince Professor McDermott that she should spend countless hours preparing an expert report (in addition to her academic duties) so that she could be subjected to a potentially grueling cross-examination in open court. Professor McDermott was up for the challenge, and as I discuss in more detail below, her evidence proved to be pivotal in the chief justice's assessment of the prohibition on polygamy.

The Significance of the Polygamy Reference

References are rather rare events in Canada. The federal government, through the governor in council, may refer to the Supreme Court of Canada for hearing and consideration important questions of law or fact (Supreme Court Act, R.S.C., 1985, c. S-26, s. 53). Each of Canada's provinces has enacted legislation that permits the provincial government to refer questions to the Court of Appeal of that province, and in British Columbia and Manitoba, the province may refer the questions either to the lower court (the BCSC in British Columbia) or to the appellate court of the province.[2] The reference procedure has been used mainly for constitutional questions (Hogg 2007) and, until the Polygamy Reference, no reference had ever been heard by a lower court in Canada. A decision rendered by a court on a reference question is considered to be an advisory opinion to government. While the black letter law seems to dictate that the court's answer to a reference question is not binding even on the

---

2. In British Columbia, the Constitutional Question Act (RSBC 1996) C. 68 governs reference questions. Section 1 permits the lieutenant governor in council to refer any matter to the Court of Appeal or to the Supreme Court of the province. In Manitoba, the Constitutional Questions Act (CCSM) c. C180 governs reference questions. Section 1 permits the lieutenant governor in council to refer any matter to the Court of Appeal or to the Court of Queen's Bench in the province.

parties to the reference and is not of the same precedential weight as an opinion in an actual case, in practice opinions rendered on a reference question are treated in the same way as other judicial judgments (Hogg 2007, 8–18).

The initiation of the Polygamy Reference at the trial court level allowed all the participants to put a comprehensive evidentiary record before the court. Unlike traditional litigation, in constitutional references there are no parties per se and there are no specific adjudicative facts. This can be a central disadvantage of references because opinions may be rendered in a factual vacuum. This problem is exacerbated by the hearing of a reference at the appellate level where there are very limited options for introducing facts. Appellate references generally rely upon affidavits filed with the court as well as the written and oral arguments of counsel. As the chief justice noted, "this limits the ability of participants to rigorously challenge their reliability" (*Reference*, para. 53).

The hearing of the Polygamy Reference in the trial court throughout the fall of 2010 and spring of 2011 avoided the factual vacuum problem, and as the provincial government had intended, it allowed the participants to "put a human face on polygamy in contrast to the more abstract nature of a reference to the B.C. Court of Appeal" (*Reference*, para. 57). The evidentiary record in reference included viva voce and written testimony from expert and lay witnesses, cross-examinations of these witnesses, video affidavits, academic studies, and commentary, as well as popular culture materials on polygamy, including documentaries, news reports, talk shows, and wonderfully titled books such as *The Ethical Slut: A Practical Guide to Polyamory* and *Open Relationships and Other Adventures*.

The parties and interveners created a diverse and wide-ranging evidentiary record that would have been impossible in a typical appellate reference. The majority of the expert witnesses as well as a number of the lay witnesses were cross-examined. While the interveners did not have an automatic right to tender evidence, cross-examine witnesses, or make oral submissions, the chief justice permitted them to do so as long as their evidence and subsequent submissions were not unnecessarily duplicative. As a result, the court received a wide range of materials and testimony that advanced the unique perspectives of each of the interveners.

There were over ninety expert reports. There were also affidavits from individuals in polygamous relationships, and twenty-two of these individuals were examined and cross-examined during the hearing phase of the proceeding. The experts were drawn from a wide range of academic disciplines including anthropology, psychology, sociology, law, economics, family demography, history, and theology, and much of their research was interdisciplinary and cross-cultural. Some experts, such as Professor McDermott, undertook original research specifically for the Polygamy Reference, while others offered case study observations from their years of clinical experience. The lay witnesses included current members of the FLDS community in Bountiful, British Columbia, who gave their written and viva voce evidence under cover of anonymity, as well as former members of the FLDS who testified in open court. Other lay witnesses described their involvement with polyamory and other types of nonconjugal relationships.

The chief justice took a liberal approach to the admissibility of evidence in the Polygamy Reference and admitted all of the evidence that was tendered. This approach allowed for a proper evidentiary foundation to be created and, in the chief justice's words, "maximize[d] the trial reference's potential in terms of creating an evidentiary record" (*Reference*, para. 46). This liberal approach was facilitated, in part, by the fact that the Polygamy Reference was not a typical civil proceeding. All the evidence was appropriately characterized as legislative or social fact evidence, and the admissibility requirements for such evidence in Canadian law are less stringent.

The Polygamy Reference was unique in that the proceeding was characterized by a high level of public access to the proceeding itself as well as the documents filed in the proceeding. One of the interveners, the Canadian Polyamory Advocacy Association, provided public access, via its website, to the vast majority of the court file, including the affidavits, written submissions, and transcripts of the viva voce evidence. This material was also physically accessible to the public in a resource library located adjacent to the courtroom. Public access was further facilitated through the Canadian Broadcasting Corporation's live webcast of the closing arguments. While the Supreme Court of Canada regularly televises its proceedings, it is relatively rare for a provincial court, especially a trial court, to do so.

The Polygamy Reference received widespread media attention in Canada, with the majority of pundits predicting that the Chief Justice would find the polygamy prohibition unconstitutional. Generally, these predictions focused on the fact that the prohibition was over one hundred years old and, as such, the prohibition was unlikely to accord with the guarantees of freedom of religion, liberty, security of the person, and equality that are now ensconced in the Canadian Charter of Rights and Freedoms. In particular, many argued that the blanket prohibition on polygamy must be overly broad because there were numerous witnesses who testified that their polygamous relationships were consensual, loving, and free from the harms traditionally associated with polygamy. According to these witnesses, there was nothing inherently harmful about the practice of polygamy, and their good polygamous relationships should not be criminalized simply because there are some individuals who exploit the practice.

The chief justice ultimately rejected these arguments and, in a judgment that was over three hundred pages long, he held that the criminal prohibition on polygamy was constitutional. He found that "while the prohibition offends both the freedom of religion of identifiable groups and the liberty interests of children between the ages of twelve and seventeen who were married into polygamy, the prohibition was demonstrably justified in a free and democratic society, save in its application to the latter group" (*Reference*, para. 15). This justification was grounded in the evidence of the harms of polygamy submitted by the attorneys general. Relying in large part on Professor McDermott's testimony, the chief justice found that there are indeed inherent harms in the practice of polygamy that justified a blanket prohibition on such relationships.

The Legal Arguments and Professor McDermott's Evidentiary Contributions

Interpreting the Criminal Code's Polygamy Prohibition

The chief justice's assessment of the constitutionality of the criminal prohibition on polygamy had first to consider how to properly interpret the text of s. 293 of the Criminal Code. Section 293 states:

293. (1) Everyone who

(*a*)   practises or enters into or in any manner agrees or consents to practise or enter into

(i)   any form of polygamy, or

(ii)   any kind of conjugal union with more than one person at the same time,

whether or not it is by law recognized as a binding form of marriage, or

(*b*)   celebrates, assists or is a party to a rite, ceremony, contract or consent that purports to sanction a relationship mentioned in subparagraph (*a*) (i) or (ii),

is guilty of an indictable offence and liable to imprisonment for a term not exceeding five years.

The AGC, the AGBC, and the amicus all offered different interpretations of s. 293, especially with respect to the meaning of "conjugal union" in s. 293(1)(*a*)(ii). The AGC argued that s. 293 prohibits practicing or entering into multiple marriages, whether they are sanctioned by civil, religious, or other means.[3] The prohibition, according to the AGC, included both polygyny and polyandry. The AGC also asserted that, given the history of the prohibition, the phrase "conjugal union" is aimed at marriage rather than mere cohabitation. The use of "conjugal union" in s. 293 is intended to capture all non–legally valid multiple marriages, including Mormon celestial marriage. The AGC argued that a "conjugal union" is not the same as a "conjugal relationship." A "conjugal union," according to the AGC, is a long-standing legal concept, used to describe a marriage, whether valid under civil law, valid only in religious law, or existing only in the view of the parties and the communities to which they belong. A "conjugal relationship," on the other hand, is a term that has recently acquired a legal meaning that did not exist at the time of the introduction of the polygamy offense. A "conjugal relationship" is now most commonly applied to a "common law relationship" or an unmarried cohabitation-based relationship.

The AGBC also focused on the "marriage" requirement and argued that the prohibition was not directed at multipartner relationships unless such a relationship had the trappings of what the AGBC called "a duplicative marriage." According to the AGBC's interpretation, multiparty

---

3. In Canada, the prohibition on bigamy is a separate Criminal Code offense.

conjugality would attract the criminal prohibition when it is or purports to be a marriage, including when it is or purports to be a pairing sanctioned by some authority and binding on its participants. In this formulation, "authority" would be some mechanism of influence, usually religious, legal, or cultural, that imposes some external consequences on decisions to enter into or remain in the relationship.

The amicus put forward the most expansive interpretation of s. 293. He argued that s. 293 criminalized all conjugality other than monogamy, regardless of gender arrangement, the manner in which the union was formed, or its benefits to the participants. The amicus submitted that the prohibition also criminalized all participants in the union, alleged wrongdoers and victims alike. He also argued that the term "polygamy" encompassed same-sex polygamy, polyandry, and polygyny. The amicus interpreted "conjugal union" as a "marriage-like" relationship or conjugal relationship that encompassed formal marriages but also included common law relationships.

The chief justice largely accepted the AGC's interpretation of s. 293 (*Reference*, para. 977). He rejected the amicus's contention that the prohibition extended to conjugal relationships or common law cohabitation (*Reference*, para. 984). Instead, the chief justice held that the focus of the provision was on multiple marriages that he described as "pair-bonding relationships sanctioned by civil, religious, or other means" (*Reference*, para. 987). He accepted that both "polygamy" and "conjugal union" referred to marriage rather than other nonsanctioned forms of relationships: "Section 293, from its first iteration, has been viewed as creating an offence relating to the law of marriage" (*Reference*, para. 999). He concluded that the offense "is not directed at multi-party, unmarried relationships or common law cohabitation, but is directed at both polygyny and polyandry. It is also directed at multi-party same sex marriages" (*Reference*, para. 1037).

Practically speaking, the chief justice's interpretation excludes polyamorists because they generally do not enter into marriages. This exclusion must have come as a relief to members of the Canadian Polyamory Advocacy Association, one of the intervener organizations in the Polygamy Reference, who had worried that their relationships could be subject to criminal sanction under s. 293.

The chief justice's narrow interpretation of s. 293 aligned well with the evidence of harms presented by the attorneys general. This evidence was focused exclusively on the harms associated with polygamous *marriages*. No evidence was offered with respect to the potential harms of other forms of multiparty relationships because neither the AGC nor the AGBC interpreted s. 293 as including those forms of relationships. The long history of the prohibition on polygamy in Western democracies demonstrated that these states, including Canada, were concerned with deterring and punishing multiparty marital structures, not multiparty cohabitation. The chief justice's interpretation of s. 293 recognized the preeminent place that the institution of monogamous marriage has taken in Western culture, and the judgment, as a whole, ought to be viewed as reinforcing the structural power of this institution in Canadian society.

The Constitutional Arguments

Once the proper interpretation of s. 293 was established, the chief justice moved on to consider the constitutionality of the prohibition. The primary constitutional argument in the Polygamy Reference was actually quite straightforward. The amicus and his allied interveners argued that the polygamy prohibition stemmed from anti-Mormon sentiment in the nineteenth century and served only to reinforce the mainstream Christian norm of monogamy. The evidence, in their opinion, did not demonstrate that polygamy itself was harmful. Rather, the harms were more accurately characterized as arising out of particular relationships or communities. The amicus and his allies argued that the polygamy prohibition violated five provisions in the Charter: freedom of religion, freedom of expression, freedom of association, liberty and security of the person, and equality.

The crux of the amicus's argument was that the blanket ban on polygamy criminalized all polygamous relationships whether or not those relationships were harmful to the individuals involved or harmful to society in general. Other Criminal Code offenses target conduct that is demonstrably harmful (trafficking in persons, forcible confinement, assault, sexual assault, and so forth), and in the amicus's submission, these laws could and should be used to deter and punish harmful conduct in polygamous relationships. There was, therefore, no need to ban all forms of polygamous relationships when we already had laws on the books that prohibit any bad conduct that may arise in such relationships.

On the other hand, the AGC as well as the AGBC and their allies argued that the objective of the polygamy prohibition was the prevention of harm and that Parliament is entitled to criminalize conduct where there is a reasoned apprehension that the conduct poses a risk of harm. The evidence, in the view of these participants, demonstrated that polygamy was associated with significant and substantial harms to individuals, especially women and children, and to society as a whole.

The attorneys general focused their arguments on establishing that the harms associated with polygamy inhered in the structure of polygamy itself and were not simply a product of particular religious or cultural beliefs. The fact that Parliament had addressed some of the harms associated with polygamy through the enactment of other Criminal Code prohibitions did not foreclose Parliament's ability to prohibit the practice itself. The attorneys general argued that this was especially true when a narrower prohibition would be ineffective in responding to the structural harms of polygamy itself.

Professor McDermott's Evidentiary Contributions

In order to counter the amicus's claim that the polygamy prohibition went too far because it captured individuals who were in consensual, loving polygamous relationships, it was crucial for the attorneys general to marshal evidence of polygamy's universal structural harms. For this reason, the evidentiary contributions of Professor McDermott were invaluable. Her evidence dispelled the notion that polygamous relationships can be easily divided into good and bad relationships and, instead, demonstrated that polygamy itself, regardless of the participants, results in a whole host of negative consequences. This was significant because in Charter litigation involving challenges to criminalized activities, the government must demonstrate a reasoned apprehension of harm (that is not insignificant or trivial) in order to justify the criminalization of the activity.

Professor McDermott and a number of other experts in the Polygamy Reference conducted reviews of the relevant literature on polygamy. This literature was extremely diverse and was drawn from almost every academic discipline including economics, anthropology, history, psychology, sociology, biology, political science, philosophy, and law. The majority of these publications came to the same conclusion: polygamy produces harmful effects, including physical and sexual abuse, psychological and mental health problems, lower levels of equality and dignity for women and children, higher rates of female and infant mortality, exploitation of young girls, economic hardship, and deprivation.

Yet, as Professor McDermott noted in her expert report, the existing literature on polygamy was limited by the scope of the investigations that were typically confined to a particular country or particular group. This literature, on its own, did not provide evidence of the universality of these harms or whether these harms could be generalized to a wider population. As Professor McDermott opined, only a statistical analysis could provide reliable information regarding how widespread or universal the relationship between polygamy and these harmful effects might be.

The AGC asked Professor McDermott to present her opinion on three issues: (1) the impact of polygamist relationships on women's equality; (2) the impact of polygamist relationships on children, including child brides and the children of polygamist unions; and (3) the impact of polygamist relationships on the nation-state (*Reference*, para. 610). The AGC requested that Professor McDermott conduct both a literature review as well as an original statistical analysis in order to answer these questions.

The most important aspect of Professor McDermott's study, for the purposes of the Polygamy Reference, was that it was a cross-cultural/cross-national study. She analyzed systemic data regarding polygyny and its relationship to dependent variables of interest regarding women, children, and the nation-state. Her data came from two principal sources: data on women and children came from the WomanStats Project Database, and data on the nation-state came from two international organizations, the Stockholm International Peace Research Institute and Freedom House. Professor McDermott's study included data from every country in the world with a population over two hundred thousand. That amounted to 171 countries or over 90 percent of the countries in the world.

Based on her knowledge of existing literature on the impacts of polygyny, Professor McDermott chose thirteen dependent variables to study, including life expectancy, birth rates, sex trafficking, domestic violence, and political and civil liberties. Professor McDermott explained in her report that these variables were chosen because they "constitute the group of outcomes theoretically hypothesized to be most likely to be affected by polygyny" (*Reference*, para. 617). Professor McDermott controlled for variables that might directly cause the outcomes she examined, and, in particular she controlled for the effects of gross domestic product (GDP). She testified in direct examination that GDP was the "monster variable" and that "if you can find a variable that still emerges significant controlling for GDP, that really means you have something" (*Reference*, para. 618).

The results of her analysis were astonishing. As levels of polygyny increased, so did negative outcomes with respect to each of the variables tested. When she was examined in-chief during the hearing, Professor McDermott took the court through a detailed PowerPoint presentation of her findings that clearly and convincingly demonstrated the harmful effects of polygyny. The wide-ranging nature of these effects was perhaps the most surprising aspect of her study. Professor McDermott's results showed that the harms of polygyny were not limited to the individual participants; rather, as polygyny increases, the discrepancy between law and practice concerning women's equality also increased, as did the differential legal treatment of women relative to men, to the detriment of women. States with higher levels of polygyny spent more money per capita on defense, and these states displayed fewer political rights and civil liberties for both men and women (*Reference*, para. 621).

Professor McDermott's statistical analysis came as close as was possible to demonstrating a causal link between polygamy and harms. When asked by the chief justice if her analysis could establish proof on a balance of probabilities, she replied that statistically significant relationships provide the foundation of causal inference and are analogous to the civil legal standard of proof. She also acknowledged that, strictly speaking, causation itself can only be properly tested through experimentation. Obviously, it would be unethical to conduct experiments to determine whether or not polygyny causes harms. Instead, Professor McDermott testified that we must look to the strength of the statistical relationship to establish that the probability that the causation relationship is untrue is very, very unlikely. In the context of the Polygamy Reference, her statistical analysis was the only evidence capable of establishing a causal relationship between polygyny and its inherent harms.

The Amicus's Challenge to Professor McDermott's Evidence

The amicus directed his strongest critique of the AGC's evidence toward Professor McDermott's statistical analysis. This is perhaps not surprising given that her evidence was the most damaging to the amicus's position that polygamy is not inherently harmful. Her objective and comprehensive statistical analysis established that rising levels of polygamy were positively correlated with rising levels of a whole host of negative consequences, and the amicus offered no evidence to directly contradict or to even call into question the veracity of her study. Instead, he appealed to the court's "common sense" and characterized Professor McDermott's findings as "abracadabra" (*Reference*, para. 629). Without contradictory evidence, the amicus could only suggest that the results of Professor McDermott's study were so astonishing they must be untrue.

The amicus also attempted to discredit Professor McDermott's analysis by suggesting that her work was tainted by the fact that she became interested in polygyny as a result of the attacks on 9/11. He argued that since other academics did not find the hypothesized link between polygyny and violence compelling, Professor McDermott's study should be seen as emanating from the academic fringes and should not be taken seriously.

The amicus's cross-examination of Professor McDermott also made it clear that he did not understand the nature of her regression analysis. A significant portion of his cross-examination was dedicated to obtaining Professor McDermott's admission that her findings could not "prove" a causal link between polygyny and various harms. Professor McDermott patiently and cogently explained to the amicus that regression analysis is concerned with understanding if a correlative link exists between dependent and independent variables and that it cannot prove causation in a manner similar to experimentation. While her analysis could not prove a causal link, it did demonstrate that because of the very strong correlations between rising levels of polygyny and rising levels of harm, the possibility that polygyny was not driving the increase in those harms was very, very low.

The Chief Justice's Assessment of Professor McDermott's Evidence

Ultimately, the chief justice rejected the amicus's arguments and found that not only had the attorneys general demonstrated a reasoned apprehension of harm, they had demonstrated "concrete evidence" of harm (*Reference*, para. 1044). The amicus's so-called commonsense approach to Professor McDermott's complex statistical analysis was specifically taken to task by the chief justice: "This approach . . . tends to both overstate Dr. McDermott's conclusions and obscure the basis of her methodology" (*Reference*, para. 626). The chief justice held that the amicus's criticism of Professor McDermott's study misapprehended the nature of her research, especially the fact that her study demonstrated aggregate effects rather than effects on a country-by-country basis. The chief justice understood that the purpose of Professor McDermott's study was to provide a statistical analysis of polygyny that contained "enough statistical variance or power to discern clear and meaningful statistically significant relationships between variables of interest" (*Reference*, para. 628).

At the end of the day, the chief justice's dismissal of the amicus's critique of Professor McDermott's analysis meant that a significant amount of weight was given to her findings. Indeed, the chief justice expressly relied upon the evidence of Professor McDermott in order to establish the structural harms of polygamy (*Reference*, para. 1045). He found that Professor McDermott's evidence supported "the reasoned view that the harms associated with the practice [of polygyny] are endemic; they are inherent" (*Reference*, para. 1045). This conclusion, in the chief justice's words, "is critical because it supports the view that the harms found in polygynous societies are not simply the product of individual misconduct; they arise inevitably out of the practice" (*Reference*, para. 1045).

The chief justice called Professor McDermott "a most impressive witness" who "gave very important evidence on the reference" (*Reference*, para. 580). He began his overview of her evidence by discussing the literature survey that she included in her expert report, and he accepted Professor McDermott's summary of the harms of polygamy that these scholarly works revealed (*Reference*, para. 583–87). More important, the chief justice devoted ten pages of his judgment to a discussion of Professor McDermott's original statistical analysis. He acknowledged that the literature review could only go so far in establishing that the practice of polygamy was inherently harmful and that, as a result, Professor McDermott's study was a key to his analysis of the harms:

> I have described the results of various literature reviews conducted by a number of experts concerning polygamy and its impacts. It is vaguely unsettling to base a potential conclusion (here, that polygamy causes harm) on an expert's review of what other alleged experts have written on the subject. That is why the original work undertaken for the reference by the AG Canada's witness, Dr. McDermott, serves such a valuable purpose in this inquiry. (*Reference*, para. 609)

The chief justice noted that "many of the empirical studies on polygamy center on cultures far removed from North America," and for that reason, "caution is urged in extrapolating findings in these studies to our situation here" (*Reference*, para. 641). Professor McDermott's expert report was critically important in establishing the cross-cultural nature of these harms. In the words of the chief justice, "these concerns [about the applicability of non–North American studies] are met in large measure, I find, by the statistical analysis of Dr. McDermott. As I have related, her data spans [*sic*] 172 countries and her analysis controlled for the 'monster variable'—GDP" (*Reference*, para. 642). Professor McDermott's study enabled the chief justice to connect the harms outlined in the literature surveys conducted by several witnesses in the Polygamy Reference to the issue before him, namely, is Canada's current prohibition on polygamy justified? Without her analysis, these additional studies were of limited utility because they could only attest to the specific historical, geographical, and cultural contexts in which they were conducted.

Professor McDermott's statistical analysis not only lent credibility (and cultural transferability) to the findings of previous social science inquiries into the effects of polygamous relationships, it also validated and lent credibility to the personal testimony of former members of the FLDS. The AGBC had located numerous individuals in Canada and the United States who were willing to come forward and tell their stories in open court. The testimony of these witnesses focused on their experience of polygamy in the FLDS community, either as wives in polygamous marriages or as children born into those marriages.

The evidence of these witnesses was, at times, graphic and shocking as they described the daily violence and control perpetuated in these relationships. The chief justice called their evidence "highly personal and very moving" (*Reference*, para. 666). These lay witnesses provided the chief justice with a compelling image of the various harms of polygamy in this particular religious community. However, just as the scholarly works that focused on non–North American experiences of polygamy could only go so far in establishing the harms of polygamy, these firsthand accounts of the harms were limited by the fact that all the relationships occurred in a particular religious community. Arguably, these harms could simply have been the product of certain religious beliefs and practices rather than polygamy itself.

The combination of the testimony of these witnesses with the academic studies and Professor McDermott's original statistical analysis was compelling and, taken together, left no doubt in the chief justice's mind that harms inhere in the very structure of polygamy itself: "What is striking is the congruity we find in the dangers of polygamy found in the African and Middle Eastern based empirical studies . . . , those predicted by Dr. McDermott's work, and those found 'on the ground' and anecdotally in North America" (*Reference*, para. 643). Professor McDermott's study demonstrated that the harms of polygyny are not dependent upon particular national, regional, cultural, or religious contexts; rather, these harms "can be generalized, and they can be expected to occur wherever polygyny exists" (*Reference*, para. 624; Hogg 2007, 8–15).

Epilogue

It's been several years since the chief justice released his decision in the Polygamy Reference. In the interim, an appeal was considered but ultimately not pursued, and investigations by the Royal Canadian Mounted Police into the situation in Bountiful, British Columbia, continued.

In August 2014, British Columbia's Criminal Justice Branch approved polygamy and child-related charges against several members of the community in Bountiful. Those charged include the leaders of the FLDS sect, Winston Blackmore and James Oler. While these prosecutions are in the very early stages, I anticipate that one or both of them will challenge the constitutionality of s. 293 as part of their defense. It remains to be seen how the Polygamy Reference will be utilized in these criminal proceedings. While technically only an advisory opinion, the chief justice's decision is based on an epic record of evidence that will be hard to ignore in any future proceedings.

References

Hogg, Peter W. 2007. *Constitutional Law of Canada*, 5th ed., vol. 1. Toronto: Carswell.
Reference re: Section 293 of the Criminal Code of Canada, 2011 BCSC 1588.

Comment 2

Polygyny, Pastoralism, and Violence against Women

Robert Jervis

Interdisciplinarity is all the rage today. University presidents brag to funders that their faculties and curricula are distinguished from those of their peers by breaking down disciplinary barriers, and therefore require and deserve further financial support, while deans nag the faculty for not being interdisciplinary enough. In this climate, it is perhaps too easy for scholars to lose sight of the value of research that is interdisciplinary. The essay by McDermott and Cowden is a marvelous illustration of the fact that we should not let our (justified) annoyance at the desire of university administrators to climb on the latest bandwagon blind us to the values of scholarship that crosses disciplinary lines.

Academic disciplines are odd things. The world, of course, does not come to us with disciplinary labels. Disciplinary lines are not entirely arbitrary; we have developed them over time because the world is much too complicated to grasp in its entirety, and we believe that our academic fields segment it in a way that does least damage to the fabric while allowing us to fruitfully specialize. Even in earlier centuries when knowledge was more limited, it is hard to believe that we could make progress without erecting boundaries and, for most of our endeavors, staying within them.

These boundaries can be excessively confining, however. They can lead us to shape the questions we ask as well as the answers we give and can divert much scholarly attention to quarrels within the discipline rather than to puzzles taken from the world. This is especially true in social science, and I think it is no accident that the disciplinary lines there have remained more static than in natural science. In the latter, new fields are created following the development of new technologies, new research findings, and new ways of thinking. New fields such as molecular biology cannot only arise but become central to both pure and applied science. Related, cross-disciplinary collaborations are common as it becomes clear that many important questions cannot be answered by the theories and tools of only one discipline.

I do not want to overdraw the contrast with social science. Significant scholarship exists at the intersection of the disciplines, for example in political economy, political psychology (now joined by economists, who have renamed this area "behavioral economics"), and political history, to name just three of those I am most familiar with. In addition, the areas of inquiry that have been shunned by most of the disciplines may become the target of attention. Lacking an obvious disciplinary home, they may be "born interdisciplinary," as I think is true for some gender and ethnic studies. Even when this does not happen, the pursuit of questions in one discipline almost automatically may lead to engagement with others. Students of international politics, especially when using qualitative tools, must engage with international history since they are seeking theories that explain conflicts that have (and have not) occurred in the past.

Concepts of course also flow across disciplinary boundaries, and much of political science incorporates standard economic concepts like collective goods and moral hazard without any second thoughts.[1] This is not to say that there are no barriers. Limits to our time mean that none of us can be as familiar with work in relevant fields as we should be. Furthermore, different disciplines, like tribes separated by mountain ranges, over time develop different vocabularies and perhaps different ways of thinking that

---

1. Indeed, sometimes the concepts are adopted without much thought, as has been the case with the idea of "costly signaling." For a critique, see Jervis 2002.

block or distort the flow of ideas. To take just one example, the spate of marvelous books marking the anniversary of the outbreak of World War I focuses on the freedom of choice and the role of decisions made by individuals without exploring the political science literature on structure and agency. More specifically, these historians argue against the powerful role of the alliances by noting that many of the decisions were influenced by the fear that allies would not remain loyal. A good point, to be sure, but one that ignores the parallel and more sophisticated international relations thinking about the role of alliances in bipolar and multipolar systems that is associated with the pathbreaking work of Kenneth Waltz (1997) that used 1914 to show that the very possibility of realignment under multipolarity can lead to policy rigidity.

Of course each of us is likely to be quicker to notice instances in which scholars from other disciplines have been insufficiently aware of areas in ours than to realize where we ourselves need to look abroad. Furthermore, we are likely to look mainly to our own discipline to generate the questions we ask.

In all these respects, the essay by McDermott and Cowden is a welcome exception. It cannot be readily classified in disciplinary terms, yet also avoids the trap of crossing field lines only by virtue of a few citations and superficial gestures. Rather, they take a problem that is generated not by a political science theory but by patterns in the world, that is important for both theory and policy, and that, partly because it is not strictly in the purview of any one discipline, remains understudied. Or, to put it more precisely, while many of the pieces that McDermott and Cowden discuss have been well analyzed by others, the connections have not been. These, combined with the analysis of an extensive data set, make very important contributions.

The connections extend in multiple directions, and I can follow only a few of them. To start with the international relations context, there is a large literature on the domestic sources of foreign policy. But this concentrates on characteristics that are familiar to political scientists, mostly whether the regime is democratic or not. Putting aside the self-congratulatory nature of much of this work that, contrary to the conventional wisdom of much of the nineteenth and twentieth centuries, sees democracies as uniquely qualified for intelligent, cooperative, and peaceful foreign policies, it seems unfortunate to relegate nondemocracies, which have constituted the overwhelming bulk of the governments throughout history, to a residual category.[2] Regardless of the strengths and weaknesses of this scholarship, it is limited by focusing on the regime characteristics that the history of great power relations over the past century have made salient to us. While these are indeed interesting and important times, we should not allow them to blinker our vision. McDermott and Cowden remind us that while government structures are important, they develop with and often reflect characteristics of our societies, which can affect external relations in a number of ways. Building on previous work,[3] they argue that polygamous societies are likely to be violent, both internally and externally. The reasons are a complex interaction among multiple factors, most of which reinforce each other. In societies that are both polygamous and pastoralist, they show, wealth is accumulated through livestock, which is hard to protect against raids. This puts a premium on having ready allies, which in turn increases the value of multiple wives because these provide for a widened kin network. Multiple children are valuable as well, not only for looking after the herds, but because when daughters are given as brides, additional connections are made or strengthened. The need for protection also enhances the salience of honor because it provides a reputation for a willingness to fight that can help deter attacks. Of course if some men have multiple wives, others will be without mates. These young men have added incentives to raid other groups and, if this is not feasible, increase the pool of men who are spoiling for a fight. The result is a political culture that is primed for violence and a psychology that is permeated by belligerence.

Political scientists are not generally sensitive to social and social psychological characteristics of this kind. They are not explicitly political in their nature, do not fit most political science theories, and are far from the dominant modes of theorizing. Although they can partly be seen in terms of incentives and strategies, concepts that come easily to political scientists, they also involve patterns of culture and ways of life that do not. An overly atomized perspective that overlooks beliefs and values that are inherently social will miss much of what is going on. In the same way,

---

2. For an excellent discussion of how different kinds of authoritarian regimes follow different foreign policies, see Weeks 2014, Hudson et al. 2008/9, and Hudson et al. 2012.

3. See, for example, Hudson and den Boer 2004.

any attempt to view this as the operation of a political system without considering the kind of society in which it is embedded will mislead.

Although social scientists have abandoned simple ideas of unilinear political modernization with the adoption of liberal Western norms contributing to and following from economic growth, we still often look first to the level of a society's wealth as a determinant of what we conceive of as dependent variables such as equal treatment for women. So it is particularly striking that the association of this unfortunate outcome with polygamy and pastoralism remains holding the society's wealth constant. Presumably at some point links between wealth and lower levels of gender violence would appear, although the causation could run both ways. That is, putting aside petrostates, it is hard to imagine a society growing very rich while keeping women subjugated. The failure to utilize the resources represented by half the population must hold societies back. Conversely, at some point the patterns and beliefs associated with a society that is growing richer are likely to change attitudes about gender roles and responsibilities. But the relationships are by no means simple, direct, and unilinear; economic success does not automatically lead to values and attitudes that we associate with liberal democracies. Neither would democracy itself necessarily produce such changes. Majority control, stable and transparent institutions, and fairly uninhibited political discussions are compatible with what we see as oppressive conditions if these are rooted in appropriate social conditions and ways of thinking. This does not mean that progress (as we would judge it) is impossible, but only that some of the straightforward if difficult paths that are familiar to us seem not to be likely.

McDermott and Cowden also show that violence tends to pervade a society. Rather than violence in some areas or against some targets substituting for violence elsewhere in the society, more frequently, societies differ in their level of violence. The violence against women in polygamous and pastoralist societies does not seem to reduce or correlate with reduced levels of violence between males. At both the social and the individual level, there does not seem to be a substitution effect and a rough quota of how much violence there will be. Rather, it seems that the two forms of force go together. This is important because it means that efforts to reduce violence against women, if successful, will not automatically lead to violence popping up in other areas. It is not like squeezing a balloon. In fact, it is likely, although not certain, that multiple kinds of violence will rise and fall together.

Related, the incentives, individual outlooks, and shared forms of socialization that produce violence against women are locked together in a system.[4] Elements may, and with polygamy combined with pastoralism, apparently do, reinforce each other in a way that is likely to produce negative or stabilizing feedback. That is, within a significant range, pressures on the system to move it in one direction will call up counterbalancing forces that produce homeostasis. I do not want to exaggerate this point. In the 1950s and 1960s, many theorists of comparative politics, borrowing from structural-functional sociology, talked too glibly about political systems that were self-stabilizing, and more recently many social constructivists assert that systems, especially of oppression, reproduce themselves without undertaking a more careful theoretical and empirical analysis that would be needed to sustain these arguments.

McDermott and Cowden are more careful and do not claim that these systems never change. But they do show why some forces, including greater education for women, may not produce the straightforward change that a simpler analysis would suggest. Indeed, changes that undermine the control by males, especially those with few prospects for success, can increase rather than decrease violence. On the other hand, they show that change is not excluded and can best and most peacefully come about through an understanding of how the parts to the system fit together and how alterations in one element or relationship can ramify more broadly. I would just add that change in a complex system is never completely predictable, in part because we are dealing with actors who have their own goals and theories of how the system works. For better or for worse, the people we are studying often outsmart us, and we need tools from as many disciplines as possible to keep up with them.

References

Hudson, Valerie M., Bonnie Ballif-Spanvill, Mary Caprioli, and Chad F. Emmett. 2012. *Sex and World Peace*. New York: Columbia University Press.

---

4. For my own perspective on the general dynamics at work, see Jervis 1997.

Hudson, Valerie M., Mary Caprioli, Bonnie Ballif-Spanvill, Rose McDermott, and Chad F. Emmett. 2008/9. "The Heart of the Matter: The Security of Women and the Security of States," *International Security* 33 (3): 7–45.

Hudson, Valerie M., and Andrea M. den Boer. 2004. *Bare Branches: The Security Implications of Asia's Surplus Male Population.* Cambridge, MA: MIT Press.

Jervis, Robert. 1997. *System Effects: Complexity in Political and Social Life.* Princeton, NJ: Princeton University Press.

——. 2002. "Signaling and Perception: Drawing Inferences and Projecting Images." In *Political Psychology,* edited by Kristen Renwick Monroe, 293–312. Mahwah, NJ: Earlbaum.

Waltz, Kenneth N. 1979. *Theory of International Politics.* Reading, MA: Addison-Wesley.

Weeks, Jessica L. P. 2014. *Dictators at War and Peace.* Ithaca, NY: Cornell University Press.

Comment 3

THE DEEP STRUCTURE OF COLLECTIVE SECURITY

Thoughts on McDermott, Smuts, and Sanday

Valerie M. Hudson

The writings of Rose McDermott and her coauthors[1] are revolutionary in their import, and their findings have profound implications for the fields of political science and international relations (IR). This commentary on the three chapters cowritten by McDermott aspires to make plain the ramifications of her research for our understandings of political order, interstate and intrastate conflict, and national security. In addition, McDermott's work is a welcome bridge between "hard science" and "soft science" approaches to understanding human behavior, which approaches are, regrettably, typically alien to one another. But first, a prefatory discussion on a foundational concept that is indispensable to our theoretical and empirical journey.

---

1. Hereafter, I will simply write "McDermott," but the reader should understand that to mean "McDermott and her coauthors," including Jonathan Cowden, Steve Fish, Danielle Lussier, and Peter Hatemi.

Sex: Can We See It or Say It Anymore?

Sex is the biological distinction between persons carrying XX or XY chromosomes. The vast majority of humankind carries one or the other of these two chromosomal configurations, though there are a very tiny percentage of individuals who carry alternative configurations, such as XXY, XXX, XYY, etc. Barring pathology, those with the XX configuration are capable of bearing children; those with the XY configuration are not, but rather genetically contribute to the conception of a child.

Gender is what we make of sexual difference. However, biological sexual difference persists no matter what one's theory of gender is. McDermott is prepared to investigate sexual difference; however, there are many others, including those who self-identify as feminist scholars, who apparently wish to stay solely in the world of gender (Sjoberg 2015). I would argue that the latter stance is not optimal for feminist IR/political science. "Women"—persons with XX sex-chromosome configurations—are beaten and abused every day because of this biological sexual difference and what is made of it. Female fetuses are being aborted by the tens of millions because they exhibit this sexual difference and what is made of it. And no matter what new techniques are developed in artificial reproduction, because sexual difference determines whether an individual can be a mother or can be a father, important experiential differences will persist between men and women. Sexual difference is real. No matter how we multiply or modify gender orientations in our postmodern world, those stubborn "two most common sex-chromosome configurations" will still be with us (Sjoberg 2015). We need to incorporate both sex and gender in our theories.

But it appears that sexual difference has become an offense to some feminist scholars on a theoretical level. That's too bad, for a feminist IR or feminist political science that ignores sexual difference and looks only at gender constructions is detached from the reality it hopes to explain and influence. McDermott takes the right stance: we must integrate our theories of gender and our theories of sexual difference. But only theorists prepared to "see" sexual difference and acknowledge that there are in reality "two most common sex-chromosome configurations," in addition to gender differences, can do this.

If some in feminist IR or feminist political science feel they must discard the entire vibrant field of feminist evolutionary biology (see, for example,

Gowaty 1992; Hrdy 2000), that is an obvious sign of theoretical mis-direction. Feminist IR/political science should be building bridges to feminists in the biological sciences, not burning them. Social scientists must be able to hold conversations with biologists about sex. In my view, McDermott's work represents progress toward this important goal, for she remains willing to examine not only gender, but sex as well, in her research.

Polygyny and Nation-State Security

McDermott and Cowden make a very strong empirical case that a pleth-ora of negative outcomes attend the practice of polygyny. Whether we speak of health outcomes, educational outcomes, nutrition outcomes, life expectancy outcomes, domestic abuse outcomes, or a variety of other human development outcomes, polygyny just degrades your collective in highly significant ways. One of the most irrational choices a society could make is legal or de facto toleration of polygyny. The empirical evidence— and not just McDermott's—is simply overwhelming that societal tolera-tion of polygyny is nuts.

But McDermott and Cowden go beyond human development and examine polygyny's association with intra- and interstate conflict also. Anthropologists have noted this association for a very long time, but IR scholars and political scientists are only now beginning to notice the same. Polygyny creates lamentable conditions not only for women and children, but also for men, for whom prevalent polygyny is the equivalent of a severe increase in the M(ale):F(emale) sex ratio. Highly masculinized sex ratios are strongly associated with higher levels of conflict, both within and between groups (Hudson and den Boer, 2004).

Polygyny produces especially unstable societies because it means that certain males in the clan will have several mates, and others may have none, undermining the solidarity necessary among the males of the group (Divale and Harris 1976; Gat 2006).[2] As Robert Wright puts it, "Extreme polygyny often goes hand in hand with extreme political hierarchy, and

---

2. Parts of the following two sections are adapted from Hudson and den Boer (2012) and Hudson et al. (2012), and used with permission.

reaches its zenith under the most despotic regimes" (1995, 98). Laura Betzig (1986), in an intriguing empirical study of 186 societies, found the correlation between polygyny and despotism to be statistically significant. Anthropologists have found significant correlation between polygyny and the amount of warfare in which societies engage (Harris 1993); Kanazawa suggests that "polygyny may be the first law of intergroup conflict (civil wars)" (2009, 32); and Boone (1983) even suggests that polygynous societies are more likely to engage in expansionist warfare as a means of distracting low-status males who may be left without mates. Richard Alexander has posited that the first evidence of transition from a clan-based foundation of society is the prohibition of polygyny:

> Because of the importance of mate competition, socially imposed monogamy exemplifies the essence of societal laws—the restricting of the ability of societal members to exercise fully their difference capacities for reproductive competition and success, and enhancing the security and potential reproductive success of the individuals who collaborate to conceive and enforce the laws. . . . There can be no doubt that there is strong correlation between nations' becoming very large and the imposition of monogamy on their citizens. It is almost as if no nation can become both quite large and quite unified except under socially imposed monogamy. This is not to say that large polygynous polities have not existed (e.g., under Islam, the Ottoman Empire) but that their numbers, sizes, unity, and durability have been less than those of large nations with socially imposed monogamy. Socially imposed monogamy inhibits the rise of the kind of disproportionately large and powerful lineages of close relatives shown by Chagnon to be involved in the fissioning of Yanomamo groups, and responsible for the development of their own set of laws and the avenging of kin. One of the correlates of the rise of nations, and a function of systems of law, is to suppress the right of responsibility to avenge wrongs done to kin, and to prevent subgroups and clans from attaining undue power. (Alexander et al. 1979, 423, 432–33)

That McDermott and Cowden find a strong statistical association between prevalence of polygyny, on the one hand, and military expenditures per capita as well as lack of political-civil rights, on the other, corroborates decades of anthropological findings in this same vein. Societies with prevalent polygyny are significantly more prone to authoritarianism as well as intra- and intergroup conflict.

That political scientists and IR specialists are only now beginning to know about these linkages is regrettable, but not unexpected—better late than never, we suppose. And McDermott is not the only IR scholar to see the link: for example, in a recent empirical piece, Mokuwa et al. (2011) show that prevalent polygyny in some West African states catalyzed rebel recruitment of low-status young men left without wives under this system, aggravating the potential for the horrific violence that engulfed nations in that region such as Sierra Leone and Liberia. Thayer and Hudson (2010) similarly find that marriage market obstruction due to polygyny and other forces makes terrorist recruitment much easier as well. McDermott's research, alongside that of others, makes it possible to say very clearly that important macrolevel state outcomes of interest to political science and IR, such as governance and conflict, are strongly influenced by the presence of prevalent polygyny.

Polygyny's Payoff: The Writings of Barbara Smuts

If polygyny is so decidedly harmful to human societies, why does it persist?

What an intriguing question—it strongly reminds me of a puzzle noted by evolutionary biologists in another species: fruit flies. In 1996, biologist William Rice reported on an experiment in which he engineered female fruit flies to be genetically static (i.e., unable to adapt). In less than fifty generations, male fruit flies evolved in what Rice termed a "sexually antagonistic" manner, resulting in "hyper-male" fruit flies that caused physical damage to the female fruit flies through their sexual behavior, significantly increasing female mortality rates (Rice 1996). This behavior did not benefit the males in any other way than mating success, and higher rates of female injury and mortality meant that offspring viability was lower. Ecological biologist Patricia Adair Gowaty calls Rice's endeavor "the most important experiment of the twentieth century" (2003, 917). Her rationale for this assessment is her conclusion that "when experimental manipulation allows one sex to dominate completely the interests of the other sex, there is catastrophe" (Gowaty 2003, 917). On the other hand, when females have reproductive autonomy, argues Gowaty, one sees lower variance in male mating success, lower female mortality, and higher offspring viability—all of which findings parallel McDermott's.

No doubt a discussion of fruit flies is unusual in an IR/political science context, but the idea that when male reproductive strategies have, as Gowaty puts it, "run amok," unintended negative consequences of broad scope result is a thesis advocated not only by those who study fruit flies, but also by those who study human evolution. For example, Potts and Hayden assert,

> Warfare, terrorism, and their attendant horrors are based on just this sort of inherited predisposition for team aggression which, whatever its origins, has become a horribly costly and counterproductive behavior in the modern world. . . . The original survival advantage enjoyed by individual males with a predisposition for team aggression has long since been replaced by a major, verging on suicidal, disadvantage for our species as a whole. . . . *To a very large extent . . . the natural tendencies of men are not consistent with the survival and well-being of their sexual partners, their children, and future generations to come.* (Potts and Hayden 2008, 25–26, 197, 301; emphasis mine)

This insight suggests that the first conflict among humans was the clash of reproductive interests between males and females. This conclusion is echoed in the work of feminist evolutionary biologists; for example, Sue Rosser asserts, "Women's oppression is the first, most widespread, and deepest oppression" (1997, 32), and Patricia Gowaty opines, "Sexist oppression is fundamental to—is 'the root' of—all other systems of oppression" (1992, 219).

The anthropologist Barbara Smuts has written perhaps most extensively on this subject; for example, she posits that "men use aggression to try to control women, and particularly to try to control female sexuality, not because men are inherently aggressive and women inherently submissive, but because men find aggression to be a useful political tool in their struggle to dominate and control women and thereby enhance their reproductive opportunities" (1992, 30). Smuts adds that "male use of aggression as a tool is not inevitable but conditional; that is, under some circumstances coercive control of women pays off, whereas under other circumstances it does not" (1992, 30). Smuts theorizes the differences have to do with how effective or ineffective female resistance to control by males is within a given collective. The more ineffective that resistance, the deeper and wider will be male dominance—and social structures and processes that systematically decrease the effectiveness of female resistance will, in general, be chosen by males for just such purposes.

Smuts hypothesizes that several near-universal social structures and processes in traditional human societies preclude effective female resistance: patrilocality is, first and foremost, a practice that deprives a woman of female kin networks that could potentially prohibit sexual coercion. It is noteworthy that McDermott also pinpoints patrilocality as a crucial variable in the polygyny–insecurity nexus, as well. Anne Campbell (2006) claims that hunter-gatherer societies adopted patrilocal mating patterns in which women left their natal families to mate with males outside their kinship system, thereby weakening natal bonds. This is the first example Smuts offers of how "male aggression has influenced not only female behavior but also the form of the social system itself" (1992, 8).

The second strategic development is the formation of male–male alliances, which aid males in the primary conflict with females. Because of patrilocality, most males in a particular area are kin, which forms a natural foundation for alliances. Smuts notes, "male reproductive strategies came to rely increasingly upon alliances with other males" (1993, 13); and "male reliance on alliances with other males in competition for status, resources, and females is a universal feature of human societies" (1992, 15).

As such fraternal alliances developed, the male dominance hierarchy structure was increasingly selected as a way to dampen male/male competition within the group. Such male dominance hierarchies were more effective in coercing women, as well as in facing threats from out-group male coalitions (or raising these other groups). These male coalitions also formed the foundation for male control of economic resources important for female reproduction. Male hunting parties would control division of game; male raiding parties would control division of spoils.

Male dominance hierarchies can, however, become extremely hierarchical, with some men controlling a vastly disproportionate share of the resources and power. Smuts hypothesizes that in such inegalitarian contexts, women will be subject to the most extreme forms of coercion, as the fear of powerful men over "the problem of imperfect monopolization of the mate" increases (Wilson, Daly, and Scheib 1997, 457). This is the game that men play with each other and that comes to overshadow all other interests, as we shall see. Powerful men with greater resources have much more to lose than poor men if their control over women is ineffective, and so they will use their resources and power to ensure they will not be losers. Smuts suggests, "The degree to which men dominate women and control their sexuality is inextricably intertwined with the degree to which some men dominate others" (1995, 18). We see, then, a link between lack of female autonomy and the rise of despotism in society.

This increasing male monopoly over the economic resources needed by females for reproduction places women in an unenviable position. It is in human societies where, especially after the development of agriculture and animal husbandry in which land and animals belonged exclusively to men, the complete economic dependence of the female could be effected (Mies 1988).

In such a state of relative prostration of human women, more effective and less costly means of sexual coercion were developed that did not require constant one-on-one violence. Indeed, Smuts (1992) argues that "gender ideology" was the first product of human speech. Men created codes of conduct for women, including marriage patterns and family law and custom, that would favor male control interests over female autonomy interests. Furthermore, they can easily coerce women to adopt and enforce such codes: "Women's adoption of cultural values that appear to go against their own interests may in fact be necessary for survival" (Smuts 1992, 26).

As McDermott's own research shows (chapter 4, this volume), in all six of the countries she and her coauthors examine, women are significantly less approving of polygyny than males—overall by a two-to-one margin. Women know firsthand the harms brought by polygyny and thus, generally speaking and also cross-culturally, oppose the system. They must be convinced by sheer survival interest, as Smuts notes, to acquiesce to prevalent polygyny, and when a societal alternative presents itself (e.g., rising social sanction of monogamy), acquiescence among women drops like a rock.

Coercion is thus necessary to effect this acquiescence. Male aggression is, then, in the first place, a strategy in the battle of the sexes, as are male alliances and other social structures and practices. Smuts suggests, "In many primates, hardly an aspect of female existence is not constrained in some way by the presence of aggressive males" (1992, 6). Furthermore she asserts, "Evolutionary analysis suggests that whenever we consider any aspect of gender inequality, we need to ask how it affects female sexuality and reproduction in ways that benefit some men at the expense of women (and of other men)" (Smuts 1995, 22).

In other words, polygyny—irrational and harmful as it is to women, children, and men—persists not only because it is effective in subordinating women's interests to men's, but also because it is advantageous in the male-on-male game of competitive advantage. That it actually detracts from the life potential of males along many dimensions is not important, for that is an absolute detraction felt by all males in a context where only relative detractions among males alone matter in the game.

Now, this is not to say that all men are aggressive, or that all men coerce females, or that such oppressive social systems are inevitable or biologically determined. Far from it. While selected, these phenomena are not genetically determined: "Culture affects phenotype, and the phenotypes of individuals in any one generation can, in turn, affect the culture encountered by the subsequent generation. Thus, an individual's phenotype is the result of dynamic interactions among an individual's genotype (genetic makeup) and the biotic, abiotic, social, and historical environment in which the individual develops and lives" (Gowaty 1992, 12).

Gowaty's observation echoes McDermott's call in the second chapter of this volume for greater attention by political scientists and IR specialists to what McDermott calls "postnatal development":

> As far as we know, not a single study in political behavior has explored prenatal conditions as predictors for later life political behavior, despite the critical importance of biological, psychological, and physiological development for all aspects of human behavior.
>
> Including developmental approaches can help us to understand how nutrition and other aspects of prenatal care can affect the propensity for violence and resilience in populations subjected to starvation, famine, or other systematic forms of stress such as forced migration. No one has yet applied the findings above to large-scale social ills such as famine and war, or examined how such effects might lead to permanent changes in brain structure and function in offspring due to malnutrition, lack of social attention, or chronic stress and fear. And these forces can be even more severe and endemic in certain regions or populations. For example, . . . the refugee situation in the Sudan represents a case where hundreds of thousands of infants and children are denied both nutrition and attention over decades.

The long-term political ramifications remain unknown. (McDermott, chapter 2, this volume)

McDermott would also be right to include on the list of "large-scale social ills" the social practice of prevalent polygyny. Prevalent polygyny is a key societal stressor, as her own research shows, and is similarly associated with nutritional deficit in women and children and also chronic stress, anxiety, and fear among mothers. (And, of course, Sudan scores a "3" on the WomanStats Polygyny Scale—no coincidence there.) How does prevalent polygyny affect "the propensity for violence" in these nations? What are the ramifications for "later life political behavior"?

Polygyny as a Canary: The Writings of Peggy Reeves Sanday

Through the research of McDermott and Smuts, we begin to glimpse a larger perspective on these issues, and anthropologist Peggy Reeves Sanday provides conceptual lenses to help us in that task. Sanday views polygyny as a canary—that is, as a signal that the society has chosen to face environmental challenges through male dominance rather than diarchy.[3] Indeed, Sanday's writings suggest that these alternative governance paradigms—male dominance or diarchy—are the only two possible political orders among human beings, and they lead to vastly different societal outcomes.

Male dominance societies, according to Sanday in her classic work *Female Power and Male Dominance* (1981), which surveys 156 tribal societies, are characterized by significant sex segregation, the exclusion of women from ritual ceremonies and social decision-making power, the view that men are the conquerors of women, attitudes that women are resources and not fully human (i.e., they are inferior to men), attitudes that women and their fertility are to be strictly controlled through patrilocality and early marriage for women, lack of property and inheritance rights for women to effect economic dependence of women on men, prevalent daughter-neglect

---

3. Diarchy refers to a system wherein males and females share power, including decision-making power, within the society. Interdependence characterizes the relationship between men and women.

(to the point of female infanticide), the valuation of "male" traits and the male–male bond and the devaluation of all things coded "female," prevalent rape/gang rape/domestic violence, and prevalent polygyny. Polygyny is a clear marker, then, of a male dominance society.

This litany of characteristics is very similar to that adumbrated by Barbara Smuts. But Sanday goes one step further. She suggests that there are also other characteristics that accompany such societies, and among them we find many of great interest to IR scholars:

- Bloodshed and war abound and are valued (Sanday 1981, 34, 35).
- The society is propelled by a deep sense of fear, conflict, and strife.
- The physical environment is viewed as dangerous and threatening, and it must be controlled and manipulated for there to be safety (Sanday 1981, 68).
- Given how driven and how dangerous a man's life is in such a society, "one is hard-pressed to say who is more oppressed—males or females" (Sanday 1981, 50). Though men think themselves "in control," their lives are governed by fear and endless competition.
- Men labor significantly less than women on a day-to-day basis (Sanday 1981, 82).
- Men's economy is based on a form of parasitism, to wit, the capturing of rents or the raiding of resources (including women) (Sanday 1981, 146).
- Male dominance societies are often characterized by an inadequate food supply or food insecurity (Sanday 1981, 200).
- Intragroup conflict abounds due to the de facto alteration of the sex ratio by polygyny (Sanday 1981, 203–4).

Food insecurity, intragroup conflict, intergroup conflict, raiding and rent-seeking with its attendant parasitism and corruption, chronic fear/conflict/strife: these are also the signs of an unstable, insecure nation-state. To choose male dominance as the governance paradigm is, then, to choose national insecurity. No wonder McDermott finds the statistical correlations she does concerning polygyny, which is a key marker that such a paradigm is ascendant.

Is there an alternative? In her survey of tribal cultures, Sanday found some that she termed "diarchic"—where women were not subordinated to men economically or physically, but were instead seen as men's equal partners. In contrast to male dominance systems, diarchies are characterized by a political system where women appoint the chiefs and hold a veto over male decision-making, where women participate in ritual ceremonies and there is no strict segregation of male and female, where there is cooperation and sharing of responsibilities between spouses, where females are understood to own the land and are not economically dependent on men, and where female infanticide and rape are all but unknown, as is polygyny.

Collective outcomes, as one might imagine, are vastly different for these societies. Sanday finds a much higher level of food security and far less intra- and intergroup conflict; she also finds that men work as much as women do, the physical environment is seen as needing protection and nurture instead of control and exploitation, and cooperation within the group is prized. While these societies that Sanday has surveyed are certainly not utopias, it is clear that diarchy, or at least moving in the direction of diarchy, is a far more sustainable foundation upon which to build a collective existence.

But McDermott has correctly identified the resulting conundrum. If children grow up under a male dominance system, there are likely to be lasting effects. If children are borne by mothers who are malnourished and full of anxiety and fear, the prenatal effects may be impossible to undo. In addition, children socialized to see all differences in hierarchic terms, and who have been shown over and over again that violence is the preferred conflict resolution technique when dealing with those who are different, are liable to internalize and act upon these legacy norms. How, then, can the reproduction of male dominance be stymied?

The longer I study these issues, the more convinced I become that family law is one important key (Hudson, Bowen, and Nielsen 2011). It is family law that encodes and justifies the originary subordination—the subordination of women to men, of mothers to fathers. The key components of that lamentable legal or customary law framework under which many women are forced to live their lives include child marriage, arranged marriage, patrilocality, no or little right to divorce for wives, custody given to the father's family, grave devaluation of daughters, lack of inheritance and property rights for women, double standards of sexual behavior for men and women where women may be killed with impunity for reasons of "male honor," the normalization of violence and rape within marriage through lack of legal restraint, and, of course, the legalization of polygyny.

When you change family law, astounding things happen, as they did in early Christian Europe when the church banned polygyny and mandated inheritance rights for wives (Hartman 2004; Goody 1983), and when the age of marriage for females rose significantly due to tenancy requirements. And it is not only in the distant past that changes to family law have served to profoundly change the character and behavior of societies. For example, at the turn of the twenty-first century, by undertaking a series of sweeping changes to family law, South Korea dismantled the deeply patrilineal system that had, among other things, caused highly abnormal sex ratios to develop in a context of fetal sex-identification technology (den Boer, Hudson, and Russell 2015). As a result, South Korea saw its sex ratio plummet to normal levels in the space of one decade, which is unprecedented in human history. While legal reform is no panacea—laws often go unenforced—changing family law seems essential to moving beyond the dysfunctional and insecure sequelae of male dominance systems. Such reform must also be accompanied by new narratives about who women are and what their relationship with men should be. As Sanday herself says, "Change the cultural plot and sex roles are conceived differently. Change sex roles and the plot will change" (1981, 12).

But there is one last question that has to be answered as well, and as yet, I have found no research on this critical topic. Indeed, one of the reasons there may be a lack of such research is that there are very few individuals, such as McDermott, who are able to bridge evolutionary biology and social science, and this question lies at that very intersection. Certainly one of the reasons that male dominance systems persist despite their disastrous outcomes for men, women, and children relates to some type of adaptation. Consider what Wrangham and Peterson have to say on the subject:

Male coalitionary violence is primal. . . . We are a part of a group within the apes where the males hold sway by combining into powerful, unpredictable, status-driven and manipulative coalitions, operating in persistent rivalry with other such coalitions. . . . This helps explain why humans are cursed with males given to vicious, lethal aggression. Thinking only of war, putting aside for the moment rape and battering and murder, the curse stems from our species' own special party-gang traits: coalitionary bonds among males, male dominion over an expandable territory, and variable party size. The combination of these traits means that killing a neighboring male is usually worthwhile, and can often be done safely. . . . Species with coalitionary bonds and variable party size—let us call them party-gang species—are wont to kill adult neighbors. (Wrangham and Peterson, 1996, 231, 233, 167–68, 165)

And these predilections are mediated by leader-selection processes within male dominance societies. Stephen Rosen postulates a concrete explanatory linkage between the logic of small gang or clan aggression and the logic of state aggression. He notes that particular societal arrangements and cultural beliefs will bring clan-minded men to positions of highest authority:

Some societies do embody values that reward strong responses to perceived challenges. This means not only that men with a higher predisposition to react strongly to challenges will be rewarded, but also that, as these men interact with each other, a cycle of reinforcing behavior would emerge that could explain . . . high levels of aggression that are provoked and sustained by perceived affronts among habitually interacting males. . . . Once established, the culture might survive its . . . origins because of institutions that inculcated and reinforced those patterns of behavior. The biological argument suggests that, in addition to those cultural factors, the ways in which members of such cultures would tend to interact with each other would produce elevated testosterone levels that would also create a self-sustaining cycle, producing individuals who are prone to [dominance behaviors]. . . . Are there societies and institutions that we would expect to select for and reinforce the behavior of high testosterone males? The answer, in theory and empirically, is that there are and have been societies and political structures that do just that. (Rosen 2005, 89–90, 95)

When we step back, we cannot help but notice the chronic insecurity of an international system founded on male dominance–organized states.

Given that male dominance systems reliably reproduce themselves and thus are not easy to forsake; given that such societies will select for leaders who play the male dominance game the most faithfully; given that male dominance systems are far and away the most frequently encountered governance type in the present international system; and given the bloody and dysfunctional sequelae of the male dominance system for men, women, and children, is there any hope for a different, more secure, and more peaceful world? Is "the tragedy of great power politics" in reality "the tragedy of male dominance," and if so, what is the answer for humankind? Even more specifically, were a diarchy to arise, how would it survive when it is surrounded by male dominance collectives intent on treating its society as prey, as an object of raiding, as a woman?

Perhaps McDermott, given her unique role as a scholar bridging the biological and the social sciences, is best positioned to apply her considerable expertise to answer these vitally important questions about humanity's future. Rose?

References

Alexander, Richard D., John L. Hoogland, Richard D. Howard, Katherine M. Noonan, and Paul W. Sherman. 1979. "Sexual Dimorphisms and Breeding Systems in Pinnipeds, Ungulates, Primates, and Humans." In *Evolutionary Biology and Human Behavior: An Anthropological Perspective*, edited by Napoleon A. Chagnon and William Irons, 402–35. North Scituate, MA: Duxbury Press.

Betzig, Laura L. 1986. *Despotism and Differential Reproduction: A Darwinian View of History*. New York: Aldine de Gruyter.

Boone, James L. 1983. "Noble Family Structure and Expansionist Warfare in the Late Middle Ages: A Socioecological Approach." In *Rethinking Human Adaptation: Biological and Cultural Models*, edited by Rada Dyson-Hudson and Michael A. Little, 79–96. Boulder, CO: Westview.

Campbell, Anne. 2006. "Sex Differences in Direct Aggression: What Are the Psychological Mediators?" *Aggression and Violent Behavior* 11 (3): 237– 64.

Den Boer, Andrea, Valerie M. Hudson, and Jenny Russell. 2015. "China's Mismatched Bookends: A Tale of Birth Sex Ratios in South Korea and Vietnam." Paper presented at the International Studies Association annual conference, New Orleans, Louisiana, 18–21 February.

Divale, William Tulio, and Marvin Harris. 1976. "Population, Warfare, and the Male Supremacist Complex." *American Anthropologist* 78:521–38.

Gat, Azar. 2006. *War in Human Civilization*. Oxford: Oxford University Press.

Goody, Jack. 1983. *The Development of the Family and Marriage in Europe*. Cambridge: Cambridge University Press.

Gowaty, Patricia Adair. 1992. "Evolutionary Biology and Feminism." *Human Nature* 3:217–49.

——. 2003. "Sexual Natures: How Feminism Changed Evolutionary Biology." *Signs* 28 (3): 901–21.

Harris, Marvin. 1993. "The Evolution of Gender Hierarchies: A Trial Formulation." In *Sex and Gender Hierarchies*, edited by Barbara D. Miller, 57–79. Cambridge: Cambridge University Press.

Hartman, Mary S. 2004. *The Household and the Making of History: A Subversive View of the Western Past*. Cambridge: Cambridge University Press.

Hrdy, Sarah Blaffer. 2000. *Mother Nature: Maternal Instincts and How They Shape the Human Species*. New York: Ballantine Books.

Hudson, Valerie M., Bonnie Ballif-Spanvill, Mary Caprioli, and Chad F. Emmett. 2012. *Sex and World Peace*. New York: Columbia University Press.

Hudson, Valerie M., Donna Lee Bowen, and Perpetua Lynne Nielsen. 2011. "What Is the Relationship between Inequity in Family Law and Violence against Women? Approaching the Issue of Legal Enclaves." *Politics and Gender* 7 (4): 453–92.

Hudson, Valerie M., and Andrea M. den Boer. 2004. *Bare Branches: The Security Implications of Asia's Surplus Male Population*. Cambridge, MA: MIT Press.

——. 2012. "A Feminist Evolutionary Analysis of the Relationship between Violence against and Inequitable Treatment of Women, and Conflict within and between Human Collectives, Including Nation-States." In *The Oxford Handbook of Evolutionary Perspectives on Violence, Homicide, and War*, edited by Todd K. Shackelford and Viviana A. Weekes-Shackelford, 301–23. Oxford: Oxford University Press.

Kanazawa, Satoshi. 2009. "Evolutionary Psychological Foundations of Civil Wars." *Journal of Politics* 71 (1): 25–34.

Mies, Maria. 1988. "Social Origins of the Sexual Division of Labour." In Maria Mies, Veronika Bennholdt-Thomsen, and Claudia von Werlhof, *Women: The Last Colony*, 67–95. London: Zed Books.

Mokuwa, Esther, Maarten Voors, Erwin Bulte, and Paul Richards. 2011. "Peasant Grievance and Insurgency in Sierra Leone: Judicial Serfdom as a Driver of Conflict." *African Affairs* 110 (440): 339–66.

Potts, Malcolm, and Thomas Hayden. 2008. *Sex and War: How Biology Explains Warfare and Terrorism and Offers a Path to a Safer World*. Dallas: BenBella Books.

Rice, William R. 1996. "Sexually Antagonistic Male Adaptation Triggered by Experimental Arrest of Female Evolution," *Nature* 381:232–34.

Rosen, Stephen Peter. 2005. *War and Human Nature*. Princeton, NJ: Princeton University Press.

Rosser, Sue V. 1997. "Possible Implications of Feminist Theories for the Study of Evolution." In *Feminism and Evolutionary Biology: Boundaries, Intersections, and Frontiers*, edited by Patricia Adair Gowaty, 21–41. New York: Chapman and Hall.

Sanday, Peggy Reeves. 1981. *Female Power and Male Dominance: On the Origins of Sexual Inequality*. Cambridge: Cambridge University Press.

Sjoberg, Laura. 2015. "Sex and Death . . . Revisited?" *RelationsInternational*, April 2, http://relationsinternational.com/sex-and-death-again/.

Smuts, Barbara. 1992. "Male Aggression against Women: An Evolutionary Perspective." *Human Nature* 3:1–44.

——. 1995. "The Evolutionary Origins of Patriarchy." *Human Nature* 6:1–32.

Thayer, Bradley A., and Valerie M. Hudson. 2010. "Sex and the Shaheed: Insights from the Life Sciences on Islamic Suicide Terrorism." *International Security* 34 (4): 37–62.

Wilson, Margo, Martin Daly, and Joanna Scheib. 1997. "Femicide: An Evolutionary Psychological Perspective." In *Feminism and Evolutionary Biology: Boundaries, Intersections, and Frontiers*, edited by Patricia Adair Gowaty, 431–65. New York: Chapman and Hall.

Wrangham, Richard, and Dale Peterson. 1996. *Demonic Males: Apes and the Origins of Human Violence*. New York: Mariner Books.

Wright, Robert. 1995. *The Moral Animal: Evolutionary Psychology and Everyday Life*. New York: Vintage.

AFTERWORD

The Easton Lectures and David Easton's Intellectual Legacy

Kristen Renwick Monroe

This is the first of the Easton Lectures, established by members of the Ethics Center at the University of California, Irvine (UCI), to honor David Easton.[1] Easton was the Distinguished Research Professor of Political Science at UCI, president of the American Political Science Association (APSA), a fellow of the Royal Society of Canada and a fellow and vice president of the American Academy of Arts and Sciences. For many years, Easton taught at the University of Chicago, eventually serving as the Andrew McLeish Distinguished Service Professor in Social Thought until he moved to UCI. Since this is the first Easton Lecture to be published, it seems fitting to say a word about why we established the Easton Lectures and why we felt it so appropriate that Rose McDermott be the honoree chosen to deliver the first Easton Lecture.

---

1. The full name of the Ethics Center is the UCI Interdisciplinary Center for the Scientific Study of Ethics and Morality.

The Importance and Legacy of David Easton

David Easton was a critical player in the behavioralist/postbehavioralist revolutions in social science, criticizing existing political science for its failure to construct coherent theories of politics and to develop systematic techniques to gather and analyze data with which to test such theories. Easton pioneered the field of empirical political theory, advocating the development of a broad conceptual framework that would be a prototype of something comparable to natural science. His arguments touch on critical themes in the philosophy of science, the relation of political science to public policy, and the postbehavioralist revolution.

Easton addressed a question at the heart of political science as a discipline: How do we define politics itself? Easton's definition of politics as "the authoritative allocation of values" and the way he built his political system on this definition revealed the strength of what he called empirical political theory and the continuing importance of integrating theoretical and empirical political science. His system's analysis of political life encouraged the adoption of a framework for political analysis that was free of traditional Western-oriented conceptual approaches and terminology in favor of asking how political systems fulfill critical functions, such as inputs of political demands and conversion of these demands into output and feedback. While this systems approach appeared in sociology and other social sciences, it was Easton who specified how it could be applied to behavioral research on politics.[2]

Easton's works restructured the conceptual landscape of twentieth-century political science and provided a fresh, new way to analyze political phenomena.[3] Easton's theory reoriented analysis of the discipline,

---

2. Easton's agenda for behavioral and postbehavioral political science first appeared in "An Approach to the Analysis of Political Systems" (*World Politics* 1957, and was reprinted in over one hundred different publications). The fully developed Eastonian theory was presented most prominently in three books: *The Political System: An Inquiry into the State of Political Science* (1953), *A Framework for Political Analysis* (1965), and *A Systems Analysis of Political Life* (1965).

3. Indeed, Easton's success is evidenced by the fact that we routinely now speak of a political system, inputs and outputs, demands, system overload, etc. without even recognizing that this vocabulary was developed as part of an underlying theory about the political world, and that Easton is the person who developed this theory. Easton's contributions extend into careful empirical work in socialization theory and political psychology, as witnessed in *Children in*

helping promote links with other disciplines and the blurring of disciplinary boundaries. (Easton agreed with Charles Merriam in advocating
social science as a single field, telling with delight how Merriam climbed
a stepladder late one night to chisel off the "s" from "Social Sciences" on
what both Merriam and Easton thought of as the *Social Science* building
at the University of Chicago.) Easton's theory attempted to simplify the
whole of the political system and account for the different factors that
explain political action. It moved the discipline away from its traditional
emphasis on constitutions and institutional or historical analysis to forge
strong bonds with other disciplines in social science, such as anthropology, sociology, psychology, and economics. In the process, Easton recon-
ceptualized our most basic assumptions and concerns in studying politics.

While David never repudiated what he took to be the cardinal virtue
of behavioralism—its commitment to looking closely at how people acted
and what they thought—his 1969 presidential address to APSA established his later criticism of a number of aspects of the behavioralist movement, including its antiquated view of science that equated the scientific
enterprise with the principles of what Easton termed "early positivism."
Unlike many champions of behavioralism (both early and late), Easton
remained attentive to many of the important developments in the history
and philosophy of science and understood how much the philosophical
bases underlying scientific methodology shift and change over the years.
He later supported the *Perestroika* movement's attempts to open the discipline to new approaches and methodologies.

Even after Eastonian systems analysis became commonplace, Easton's
intellectual legacy continued to inspire for both its breadth and its depth. Is
there a human nature on which we should construct our scientific theories
of political life? What is the role of culture in shaping any such nature? In
molding our political potential? Does political science have a central core,
some unique definition and conceptualization of the political that sets it
apart as a discipline, separate and distinct from other branches of social
science? How objective and value-free is our work? Is it science? Are there

the Political System: Origins of Political Legitimacy, with Jack Dennis (1969). Easton's work
was critical in the development of behavioral and postbehavioral analysis, and in establishing empirical political theory as a body of work in which theories of political life were examined and tested using empirical data in a more systematic manner than had heretofore been
the case.

intrinsic and significant differences between the microlevel analysis of rational choice theory and individualist theories of human behavior, on the one hand, and the macrolevel assumptions that need to be made when we discuss collective behavior, on the other? Is it intellectually valid to speak of collective entities, such as "the state," as if they exist apart from the separate individuals that constitute them? These are just some of the questions raised by Easton's work.

Easton had an unusual capacity to ask serious questions as a way of forcing others to think more clearly about what they were doing and why it mattered. Always interested in the work of his colleagues, Easton nonetheless rarely, if ever, tried to suggest that others should follow in his research direction.

This lack of pretension was especially impressive given Easton's monumental position in political science. Easton's central contribution—the development of a value-free and culturally unbounded vocabulary of politics that he then constructed into a general theory concerning the political system—constituted an intellectual innovation that enabled scholars working primarily from an institutional and process perspective to become genuinely abstract and theoretical. Once the best-selling political science texts in the world, Easton's books proved invaluable for scholars working in comparative politics. His works freed scholars from the established Western historical frameworks and made it possible to think in strictly comparative ways, employing an abstract model. His work remains vital and intellectually alive, as political science grapples with issues of deconstructionism, postmodern political theory, and interpretive theory. It continues to be relevant for all social scientists concerned with the process by which we construct value-free comparisons that can move across cultures.

Even as Easton promoted the development and application of proper scientific methods of political inquiry that would yield rigorous and reliable knowledge of political phenomena, he also was deeply concerned about the obligation of political scientists to engage urgent issues of public policy and to illuminate disputes about the nature and implications of political values. In his influential 1969 presidential address, delivered during the rapidly escalating social and political turmoil of the late 1960s, Easton defended both these commitments with characteristic intellectual force and courage. Easton's APSA presidential address remains among the most important APSA presidential addresses delivered and inaugurated an important shift in academic political science.

Along with reforms instituted by Easton as president of the APSA—such as the establishment of the first committees on the status of women and other minorities—Easton's Presidential Address ushered in a change in APSA orientation, one that arose from a deep discontent with the direction of extant political research. Easton thus lent credibility and support to political scientists who advocated more attention to the discipline's public responsibilities and to relevant research on contemporary political problems and issues. Such a welcoming response on the part of the APSA establishment helped prevent the fracturing of the professional political science community, an outcome suffered by other professional associations at that time.

The Easton Lectures by Rose McDermott

The lectures established in Easton's honor build on this tradition. We have deliberately chosen work that is more broadly based than is the usual political science, knowing that Easton's conceptualization of "the political" includes problems and questions not always deemed relevant by more establishment-oriented political science. Our emphasis in choosing the Easton Lectures has been to find excellent scholars who follow the Eastonian tradition of challenging existing orthodoxy to produce creative and cutting-edge work, even—perhaps especially—when that work is controversial. No one could be better suited for the inaugural Easton Lecture than Rose McDermott.

Rose McDermott is the David and Mariana Fisher University Professor of International Relations at Brown University and a fellow in the American Academy of Arts and Sciences. She received her PhD (political science) and MA (experimental social psychology) from Stanford University and has taught at Cornell, the University of California at Santa Barbara (UCSB), and Harvard. She is the recipient of a Foreign Policy Analysis Distinguished Scholar Award from the International Studies Association, a past fellow of both the Radcliffe Institute for Advanced Study at Harvard University and the Stanford Center for Advanced Study in Behavioral Sciences, the latter where she currently serves on the advisory board. She has been a fellow at the Kennedy School of Government at Harvard and the recipient of the Erik Erikson Award for Early Career Achievement, given by the International Society of Political Psychology, which later elected her president.

McDermott's substantive work follows the interdisciplinary tradition espoused by Easton. McDermott focuses on political psychology and international relations, with special emphasis on decision making, emotions, and the evolutionary biological foundations of political attitudes and behavior. Her work itself is presented in seven books, some two hundred book chapters and articles, over two hundred presentations, and numerous book reviews. Her substantive work can be broken into three related periods and topics.

The first period is comprised of years spent with Amos Tversky, who was on McDermott's dissertation committee, in the late 1980s at Stanford University. Tversky's genius is well known, and his influence on McDermott is evident in the way McDermott writes about a range of topics, both psychological and military. McDermott wrote her dissertation on prospect theory, producing a model of risk taking under conditions of uncertainty, a field that Tversky developed with Daniel Kahneman and for which Kahneman won the Nobel Prize in Economics in 2004. McDermott was one of the first political scientists to apply this model in international relations. *Risk-Taking in International Relations: Prospect Theory in Post-War American Foreign Policy* (1998) examined postwar American foreign policy from the perspective of individual leaders making calculations of gains and losses in their decisions. This was followed by her broader work analyzing the importance of political psychology for international relations (*Political Psychology in International Relations*, 2004) and by her work on how illness influences presidential decision-making in foreign policy (*Presidential Leadership, Illness and Decision Making*, 2007).

McDermott's second body of work reflects her work at the Center for Evolutionary Psychology at UCSB. This experience built on McDermott's earlier work on the biological aspects of decision making but shifted the course of her inquiry into the foundations of emotion, decision making, and politics by providing her with a powerful and parsimonious theory of evolution that continues to guide her inquiry into these topics. While her edited volume (*Measuring Identity: A Guide for Social Science Research*, 2009) shows elements of this shift, McDermott's work during this period is best captured in an article from this period, written with Jamie Fowler in an attempt to reconcile Tversky's approach with the evolutionary approach. "On the Evolution of Prospect Theoretic Preferences," published in the *Journal of Politics* in 2008, remains an extremely popular and frequently downloaded work in the field.

The latest stage of McDermott's work focuses on research asking how the models and methods derived from behavior genetics can inform our understanding of individual variance in complex social and political behaviors. In this work, reflective of Easton's concern that academic work remain politically relevant, McDermott combines what she learned about the universals of human behavior from evolutionary modeling with the study of the unique and specific ways in which individuals vary, as revealed in genetic modeling. In so doing, McDermott drew on all the diverse strands in her fifteen years of training and experience in political psychology to erect an intellectual scaffolding strong enough to explain the political implications of the new behavior genetics work. This work allowed McDermott to engage in a fresh line of research, work that has now changed the direction of her professional agenda and set her at the forefront of work in social science in this area.

McDermott's work in this area challenges some of the central assumptions that have undergirded the field of political behavior for fifty years and has ripple effects far beyond the disciplinary boundaries of political science. Scholars in genetics and psychology are beginning to engage with political variables in new ways as a result of the findings on the heritable aspects of political preferences that are occurring at the intersection of politics and genetics. While controversial to some, these biological approaches are generating new models and understandings within McDermott's primary discipline of political science and have the potential to cascade through the broader intellectual community outside political science as well. For example, the volume McDermott edited with Pete Hatemi examines endogenous approaches to political attitudes and behavior. This book, *Man Is by Nature and Nurture a Political Animal: Evolution, Biology and Politics* (2011) provides a comprehensive overview of this new line of research and is designed to train and inspire new generations of students to consider undertaking further work in this area.

McDermott's current research continues to concentrate on the application of methods drawn from behavior genetics, combined with theories derived from evolutionary psychology, to explore the biological bases of complex human political and social behavior. Using both twin studies and experimental methods, McDermott has explored these factors in a number of different publications and manuscripts, some published, some under review, still others under construction.

One of the most important ways in which McDermott pursues her work in general is through the use of experimental methods, with several coauthors. One set of experiments, for example, examines how people utilize physical information, such as odors and voices, to make assessments about others' political beliefs. In addition, McDermott is involved in a series of experiments using eye tracking to examine ideological, verbal, and sex differences in attentional patterns. McDermott is currently undertaking an experiment on the effect of reciprocity on force escalation using a behavioral measure. Such work falls in line with Easton's admonition to move boldly beyond existing interdisciplinary boundaries.

All of this work relates closely to international relations, McDermott's home field, and suggests how she is making new inroads in our understanding of conflict and conflict resolution. The behavior that underlies and motivates all her work revolves around the kind of physical aggression that is involved in all kinds of conflict, terrorism, and war. Because McDermott studies this from the individual level of analysis, her approach takes on a scientific foundation not found in other works in this field. Indeed, virtually all McDermott's work remains focused on those forces, however distal or proximate, that exacerbate or ameliorate the prospects for violence across individuals and states. The importance of this seems self-evident; there is no behavior more central to the study of international relations and conflict resolution than the control and implementation of violence.

The current volume ably illustrates the importance of McDermott's work for ethics and international relations, with McDermott finding that even educating women is not enough to free them from the bondage of polygyny. Her chapters spell out the evils of polygyny. Her work—especially the chapter with Pete Hatemi—illustrates Easton's concern with broadening the type of methodological work we do and suggests how the way in which we analyze a problem can influence the substantive conclusions we reach.

We are deeply honored to present Rose McDermott's work as the first Easton Lecture. Later lectures, to be published by Cornell University Press under the superb editorial guidance of Roger Haydon, include a series of talks on British colonialism and imperialism, presented by Pulitzer Prize–winning historian Caroline Elkins, and a volume on diversity, inclusions, and marginalization and their importance on political science as a discipline. This third volume includes chapters by Rodney Hero, Matthew Holden, David Lake, Jane Mansbridge, Dianne Pinderhughes, Denise Walsh and Carol Mershon, and Laurel Weldon, inter alia.

Acknowledgments

Rose notes that this project would not have been possible without the continuing guidance, support, and intellectual inspiration of Richard Wrangham, and she is very grateful to him for the constancy of his encouragement and dedication. Rose also wishes to express her gratitude to the people in the office of the Attorney General of Canada, especially Joanne Kleinberg, B. J. Wray, and Keith Reimer. Their professional dedication is constantly inspiring. Rose thanks Valerie Hudson for providing her the opportunity to join the WomanStats project, without which the data collection essential for this project's completion would not have been possible. Rose appreciates Kristen Monroe's intrepid championing of this project; without her suggestion, this book would not have come to fruition.

It has been Kristen's great pleasure to work closely with Rose McDermott on this project. Kristen thanks Rose for delivering the first Easton Lectures. Kristen acknowledges the Easton family, the Department of Political Science at the University of California, Irvine, and the UCI Interdisciplinary Center for the Scientific Study of Ethics and Morality for their support of the Easton Lecture series. Finally, Kristen appreciates the assistance of Edna Mejia in preparing the manuscript.

Both author and volume editor would like to acknowledge and thank the wonderful people at Cornell University Press for making the entire process so seamless, especially Roger Hayden, whose editorial suggestions made the book much stronger, and Sara Ferguson, who made the text much more readable. All errors remain our own.

About the Authors

Valerie M. Hudson is professor and George H. W. Bush Chair in the Bush School of Government and Public Service at Texas A&M University. Prior to coming to Texas A&M, Hudson was a professor of political science at Brigham Young University for twenty-four years. Recipient of an Andrew Carnegie Fellowship and a Fulbright Distinguished Chair Fellowship at Australian National University, Hudson was vice president of the International Studies Association (2011–12), is a founding editorial board member of *Foreign Policy Analysis*, and also serves on several other editorial boards.

Hudson's research foci include foreign policy analysis, national security policy, social science methodology, and gender in international relations. Hudson has (co)written or (co)edited several books, including *Culture and Foreign Policy* (1992); *Bare Branches: The Security Implications of Asia's Surplus Male Populations* (2004); *Foreign Policy Analysis: Classical and Contemporary Theory* (2006); *Sex and World Peace* (2012); and *The Hillary Doctrine: Sex and American Foreign Policy* (2015). Hudson is

the cofounder of the WomanStats Project, which develops empirical arguments concerning the relationship between the security of women and the
security of the nation-states in which they live. Hudson's research, which
has appeared in journals such as *International Security* and the *American
Political Science Review*, has been funded by, among others, the National
Science Foundation, the Minerva Initiative of the U.S. Department of
Defense, and the Compton Foundation.

Robert Jervis is the Adlai E. Stevenson Professor of International Affairs
at Columbia University, and a member of the faculty since 1980. Jervis
works on perceptions and misperceptions in foreign policy decision making. Best known for two books in his early career, he also wrote *System
Effects: Complexity in Political and Social Life*. With *System Effects*, Jervis established himself as a social scientist as well as an expert in international politics. Many of his latest writings are about the Bush doctrine, of
which he is highly critical. Jervis is coeditor of the Cornell Studies in Security Affairs, a series published by Cornell University Press, and a member
of numerous editorial review boards for scholarly journals. Jervis received
his BA from Oberlin College and his PhD from the University of California, Berkeley. He has taught at Harvard University and the University
of California, Los Angeles, and was elected president of the American
Political Science Association. Jervis is a member of the American Association for the Advancement of Science and the American Academy of Arts
and Sciences. Jervis was the recipient of the 1990 University of Louisville
Grawemeyer Award for Ideas Improving World Order. In 2006 he was
awarded the NAS Award for Behavior Research Relevant to the Prevention of Nuclear War from the National Academy of Sciences.

Kristen Renwick Monroe is Chancellor's Professor of Political Science at
the University of California, Irvine (UCI), where she is the founder and
director of the UCI Interdisciplinary Center for the Scientific Study of Ethics and Morality and the associate director of the Program in Political
Psychology. She is a political psychologist, with sixteen single-authored
or edited books and awards that include five American Political Science
Association best book awards/honorable mentions and career awards
from the American Political Science Association and the International
Society of Political Psychology; she has served as president of the latter
and vice president of the former. Her work on altruism and moral choice

deals with a central problem in politics and ethics: our treatment of others. Her most recent books are *On Ethics and Economics: Conversations with Kenneth Arrow* (2016) and *A Darkling Plain: Stories of Conflict and Humanity during War* (2014). Recipient of the 2018 Berlin Prize, Monroe will spend the spring of 2018 at the American Academy in Berlin, where she will work on a book on Jewish émigrés from the Third Reich and will edit her father's letters from World War II.

B. J. Wray is legal counsel with the Department of Justice Canada in the British Columbia Regional Office. Wray specializes in constitutional law and cases involving challenges brought under the Canadian Charter of Rights and Freedoms. In addition to the Polygamy Reference, Wray has been involved in a number of high-profile Charter cases, including a challenge to Canada's prohibition on physician-assisted suicide and a challenge to Canada's medical marijuana laws. Wray holds a PhD in English Literature and prior to obtaining a law degree held a postdoctoral fellowship at the University of California, Berkeley, in the Department of Theater, Dance, and Performance Studies. She also taught various literature courses at the University of California, Davis.

Coauthors with McDermott

Jonathan Cowden received his BA in political science from Princeton, where he worked closely with Fred Greenstein on studies of Adlai Stevenson. He has a PhD in political science from Yale, where he worked with Don Green on racial bias and inequality in voting. Cowden has taught at the University of Miami, Cornell, and the University of California, Santa Barbara, and is the author of over twenty articles and book chapters.

Michael Dickerson holds a PhD in political science from Brown University.

Steve Fish is a comparative political scientist who studies democracy and regime change in developing and postcommunist countries, religion and politics, and constitutional systems and national legislatures. He is the author of *Are Muslims Distinctive? A Look at the Evidence* (2011), which was selected for *Choice*'s Outstanding Academic Titles, 2012: Top 25 Books. He is also author of *Democracy Derailed in Russia: The Failure of Open Politics* (2005), which was the recipient of the Best Book Award of 2006, presented by the Comparative Democratization Section of the American Political Science Association, and *Democracy from Scratch: Opposition and Regime in the New Russian Revolution* (1995). He is coauthor of *The Handbook of National Legislatures: A Global Survey* (2009) and *Post Communism and the Theory of Democracy* (2001). He served as a Senior Fulbright Fellow and visiting professor at the Airlangga University, Surabaya, Indonesia, in 2007, and at the European University at St. Petersburg, Russia, in 2000–1. In 2005, he was the recipient of the Distinguished Social Sciences Teaching Award of the Colleges of Letters and Science, University of California, Berkeley.

Peter K. Hatemi is Distinguished professor of political science, microbiology, and biochemistry at Penn State University. Trained at the University of Nebraska in political science and at the Queensland Institute of Medical Research in genetic epidemiology, Hatemi did postdoctoral studies in human genetics, psychiatry, and psychology at Virginia Institute for Psychiatric and Behavioral Genetics at the University of Virginia's Medical College. Hatemi is interested in political attitudes, ideology, cognition, decision making, the role of emotion in political psychology, socialization, and terrorism and political violence.

Danielle Lussier teaches political science at Grinnell College. Her research examines democratization, political behavior of former authoritarian regimes, and leadership, with a special focus on Eurasia and Indonesia. Her work has appeared in *Problems of Post-Communism, Post-Soviet Affairs,* and *Slavic Review.* She is completing a book on political participation and regime change in post-Soviet Russia and post-Suharto Indonesia. Lussier also is working on a collaborative project examining variation in social and political attitudes between Muslims and Christians around the world.

INDEX

CPSIA information can be obtained
at www.ICGtesting.com
Printed in the USA
BVOW09s0915120418
513157BV00001B/51/P